How I Learned to
Understand the World

Also by Hans Rosling

Factfulness
(with Ola Rosling and Anna Rosling Rönnlund)

How I Learned to Understand the World

* A Memoir *

Hans Rosling

with Fanny Härgestam

Translated from the Swedish
by Anna Paterson

FLATIRON
BOOKS
NEW YORK

First published in the United States by Flatiron Books,
an imprint of St. Martin's Publishing Group

HOW I LEARNED TO UNDERSTAND THE WORLD. Copyright © 2017 by
Rosling Education AB. English translation copyright © 2020 by Dr. Anna Paterson.
All rights reserved. Printed in the United States of America. For information,
address Flatiron Books, 120 Broadway, New York, NY 10271.

www.flatironbooks.com

Library of Congress Cataloging-in-Publication Data is available upon request.

ISBN 978-1-250-26689-7 (hardcover)
ISBN 978-1-250-79485-7 (international, sold outside
the U.S., subject to rights availability)
ISBN 978-1-250-26690-3 (ebook)

Our books may be purchased in bulk for promotional, educational,
or business use. Please contact your local bookseller or the Macmillan
Corporate and Premium Sales Department at 1-800-221-7945, extension
5442, or by email at MacmillanSpecialMarkets@macmillan.com.

Originally published in Sweden in 2017 under the title
Hur jag lärde mig förstå världen by Natur & Kultur

The cost of this translation was defrayed by a subsidy from the Swedish
Arts Council, gratefully acknowledged.

First U.S. Edition: 2020
First International Edition: 2020

10 9 8 7 6 5 4 3 2 1

Contents

Foreword
by Agneta Rosling

After more than fifty years of friendship and marriage, three children and eight grandchildren, Hans left me to a severe silence. Through this book his voice can be heard again.

Hans started writing about his life several years ago. He wanted to use his own family experience to tell the story of social development: to point out the similarities between the lives of people from his grandparents' generation, born in Sweden over one hundred years ago, and the lives of people in many countries today, far away from modern-day Sweden both in kilometers and in their living conditions. He wanted to share the stories that had changed or strengthened his vision of what was important in life: of what has to be changed in the world to give us all a sustainable future.

Hans always emphasized that he wasn't being altruistic when he emphasized the need for equality to avoid conflict and war, but selfish. He wanted a world without war for himself, his family and everyone else. Neither was he an optimist, because he never thought the changes he was talking about would be easy to achieve. He called himself a "possibilist" and always strived to convince his audience that it was possible to make the world a place where everyone had a fair chance of living a life on reasonable terms.

Cross-country running was a favorite sport, and Hans always liked to use a map to know where he was and a compass to find the way. This illustrates his way of analyzing any situation. You can find the right direction and reach your goal only if you know

where you are now and how things are around you. The importance of developing critical thinking habits to understand global
development is covered in greater depth in the book Hans wrote
with our son Ola Rosling and daughter-in-law Anna Rosling
Rönnlund, *Factfulness*.

This book, *How I Learned to Understand the World*, tells Hans's
own story, from childhood through to his adult life and career. It
was first published in Swedish the year Hans passed away. In this
edition, some of the stories are left out, as we thought these would
only be interesting in the Swedish context or because they had
already been told in *Factfulness*. I am very pleased that English-
language readers will be able to read Hans's memoir in this edited
form.

Hans's legacy is maintained and developed by the Gapminder
Foundation and, in various ways, by a number of universities both
in Sweden and elsewhere. Through the Gapminder Foundation,
Ola and Anna are continuing their creative work of promoting
a fact-based worldview that is easy to understand. At this time,
with the Covid-19 pandemic threatening to increase poverty and
hunger in many low-income countries, Hans would have been
more committed than ever to this work. I am satisfied to know
that his voice is still being heard, and that so many people have
learned the lessons he was trying to teach and taken his experience to heart.

Hans would have loved to test your knowledge.

The importance of a fact-based understanding of the world is
more pressing than ever.

Agneta Rosling
Uppsala, April 2020

Introduction

On February 5, 2016, I spoke to my doctor on the phone. What he said meant that writing this book became a priority. I had been prepared for bad news, and it was. The diagnosis was pancreatic cancer.

Our talk that Friday afternoon only confirmed what had gradually become obvious to me during the last few days of undergoing medical investigations. The prognosis was bad. I had approximately one year left to live.

I spent most of that evening in tears. I was lucky to have Agneta, my wife, who had been my lovely young girlfriend and then became my partner for life when we got married in 1972. Through the comfort she offered me and the support of our children and friends, I was able to adjust to this new reality. I would not die in the coming month. Terminal illness or not, life would go on. And I would be around to enjoy life during the spring and summer at least.

Cancer made the structure of my daily life unpredictable and my work schedule had to change. Just a few days after learning of my illness, I canceled all my lecture engagements and also my participation in film and TV projects. It was sad but I had no choice. Besides, I had specific plans, which helped me cope with these dramatic measures. One item on my to-do list moved to the top: complete the book that I had planned to write jointly with my son, Ola, and his wife, Anna. We had agreed on the title: *Factfulness*. Over the last eighteen years, the three of us had been working together in public education and founded a not-for-profit venture called Gapminder.

In the autumn of 2015, Anna and Ola had formulated the concept behind the book as well as its title. We had decided to set aside the following year for writing it, in parallel with our work for Gapminder. After my cancer diagnosis I was in even more of a hurry.

I quickly realized that there was enough material for two books. While *Factfulness* is about the reasons why people find development on a global scale so hard to grasp, this book is about me and how I reached that understanding.

In other words, this is a memoir. Unlike *Factfulness*, it is very short on numbers. Instead, I tell stories about meeting people who opened my eyes, and made me step back and think again.

Hans Rosling
Uppsala, January 2017

From Illiteracy to Academic Excellence

When my father came home from work in the evening, he always smelled of coffee. He worked in the roasting shed at Lindvalls Kaffe in Uppsala. This is how I came to love the scent of coffee long before I began to drink it. I often watched out for Pappa coming home from work, waiting outside as he cycled along the street. He would jump off his bike and hug me and then I'd ask him the same question every time: "Did you find anything today?"

When the sacks of green coffee beans arrived for roasting, the beans were tipped out onto a conveyor belt and, first of all, screened by a powerful magnet. The idea was to remove any metal objects that might have ended up in the sack during the drying and packing process. Pappa would bring these things home to me and tell me a story about every one of them. These stories were thrilling.

Sometimes he brought a coin. "Look, this is from Brazil," he might say. "Brazil produces more coffee than anywhere else."

My father would let me sit on his lap, open the world atlas in front of us and begin telling the story: "It's a large country and very hot. This coin turned up inside a sack from Santos," he would explain, pointing at the Brazilian port city.

He would describe the working men and women, links in the chain that ended with people in Sweden sipping their coffee. Early on, I realized the coffee pickers got the poorest pay.

Or it might be a coin from Guatemala. "In Guatemala, white Europeans own the coffee plantations. The locals, who were the first to settle in the country, only get the low-paid jobs. Like picking coffee berries."

I remember especially well the time he brought home a copper coin, a 5-cent piece from British East Africa—now Kenya—with a hole in the middle.

"I think a man would carry his coins by threading a leather strap through the holes and tying the strap around his neck. While he was spreading the coffee beans to dry on the sandy ground before putting them in the sack, perhaps the necklace broke. He picked up as many coins as he could but missed this one. It ended up among the beans and now it belongs to you."

To this day, I have kept the coins my father gave me in a wooden box. The East African coin led him to explain to me about colonialism. At the age of eight, I learned about the Mau-Mau freedom army and its demand for Kenyan independence.

My father's stories convinced me that, to him, the Latin American and African people who picked, dried and packed coffee were his colleagues. And I have no doubt at all that my powerful longing to understand the world began with Pappa telling me about the coins in the coffee sacks and showing me all those countries in the atlas. This longing grew into a lifelong passion and, later, into what I saw as my most important professional calling.

In retrospect, I realize that my father saw the worldwide rebellions against colonialism in the same way as the European struggle against Nazism. During our long weekend walks in the forest, he would talk in detail about the history of the Second World War.

Politically, my parents were no extremists. Rather the opposite; they were almost boringly ordinary. My father admired everyone who fought for justice and freedom but both of them objected just as much to the far left as to the far right.

I grew up without a religion but with a strong set of values from my parents: "Whether people do or don't believe in God isn't important, what counts is how they treat their fellow men." And: "Some people are church-goers, others take walks in the forest and enjoy nature."

Skiing with Dad

We had a small wireless set in a varnished wooden case. It stood on the String shelf above the kitchen table. During supper, we would always listen to the news from Sveriges Radio, the national broadcaster. My parents' views mattered to me as a boy, more than the actual news stories. Mamma usually commented on the Swedish news, while Pappa focused on news from abroad and often responded strongly, pausing his meal and sitting bolt upright as he listened, shushing me and Mamma. Afterward, we would talk for a long time about what we had heard.

Once, I nearly drowned in the open drain running in front of my grandparents' home. It is my earliest memory. I was just four years old and had slipped out of the garden and started to wander between the fence and the drainage channel. The channel brimmed with wastewater, a mixture of last night's rainfall and stinking sewage from neighboring homes.

Something caught my attention down there in the muck. I was curious and climbed into the drain to see better. Then I slipped. The sloping sides offered no handholds. I couldn't breathe. Everything was dark. Panicking, I tried to twist but only sank deeper into the sludge.

My nineteen-year-old aunt, who had come to look for me, spotted my kicking feet and hauled me out. When my grandma Berta took over and carried me into the kitchen, my relief was huge: to this day I still vividly remember the feeling. Grandma had been heating water on the wood-fired kitchen stove, preparing to do the dishes. Now she poured the warm water into the tin bath instead. She tested the temperature with her elbow while I undressed, then helped me into it and washed me from top to toe with a soft sponge and plenty of soap. Soon I was playing happily with the sponge. It was only many years later that I realized quite how close I had been to death.

Even then, in 1952, there was no deep drainage system in the Eriksberg area of Uppsala, where many factory workers, including my paternal grandparents, had their home. At the age of four, I had been sent to stay with my grandparents because my mother had come down with tuberculosis and been admitted to the hospital. My father visited my mother every evening after work and could only be with me on Sundays. Grandma, who had brought up seven children of her own, looked after me all week. Her youngest two were nineteen and twenty-three years old, and still living at home when I became Grandma's eighth child.

Both my paternal grandparents had been born and bred in the countryside but had eventually joined the growing urban work-force. My grandfather worked in the same Uppsala brickworks, Uppsala-Ekeby, his entire adult life. He was a kind, hardworking man who loved his wife and showed it. He and his sons had built their wooden two-story house in the evenings after work and in any other spare moment. It was his pride and joy. Thanks to an in-house mortgage plan run by the brickworks, he had been able to buy a wooded plot at the edge of the city. It became part of a housing area for factory workers.

The tall pines on the site had provided most of the construction material for Grandpa Gustav's house. He spent one summer felling the pines and sawing them into planks using a two-handed timber saw, a period of very hard labor that he remembered for the rest of his life.

Grandpa had wanted the house to be as modern as he could possibly afford but, like all working-class housing, the standard of hygiene was poor. The tap above the sink in the corner of the kitchen was the only source of running water. The sink was also where we emptied our chamber pots from the bedroom, including my small potty. The ditches that wound their way along the area's dirt roads were filthy, unhealthy open drains. Grandma kept the house and garden clean and tidy but, in the summers, the stench from the ditches was everywhere. When, later in life, I traveled to many corners of the world, the slum smell of open drains always reminded me of my summers with my grandparents.

My parents, like my grandparents, were also poor. Despite being short of money, they and their families were not seen as deprived. During my childhood and youth, household incomes and health improved steadily throughout Sweden. The health service, part of an expanding welfare state, meant that new medicines were available free of charge. My mother's tuberculosis was cured. Deaths due to infectious diseases declined sharply and accidents replaced infections as the most common cause of death in childhood. Standing pools of water near homes, like the ditch I fell into, could be fatal for my generation of Swedish children.

I was only a teenager when I became fascinated by the challenge of truly understanding how people lead their lives. I began to ask my mother's and father's parents detailed questions about their living conditions. Nothing has proved more helpful for my understanding of our modern world than examining the parallels between our world today and the worlds of my relatives in earlier generations.

Grandma Berta told me about how she and Grandpa Gustav, as newlyweds in 1915, had moved into their first home, a rented house in the countryside near Uppsala. It had a wooden floor but only one room and a kitchen. Their simple source of light was a paraffin lamp and Grandma had to fetch water from a nearby well. After twelve years and five childbirths, they could finally move closer to where Gustav worked, but their second home was also very small—a mere twenty-four square meters—and it, too, only had one room and a kitchen. However, it was supplied with electricity and piped water. Berta gave birth to their sixth child during the three years they lived there. She and Gustav and two of the children slept in the kitchen and the other four shared the single room. Grandma Berta would speak warmly about the huge difference electric light had made to their lives. It affected everything, including how she ran the household and how the children did their homework. Importantly, if someone fell ill during the hours of darkness, the light could be switched on. Her praise of electricity was unstinting.

The family had to use outdoor latrines—holes in the ground—in their first two homes. In 1930, when they moved into the house Grandpa had built, an indoor latrine had been dug in the cellar. The new house had four rooms, all wired for electric light. Even by 1952, though, when I was staying with my grandparents, Grandma used the wood-fired stove for cooking, heating water for washing and laundry, and so on. That year, they got their first telephone.

Grandpa had also installed a tap in the cellar and placed two large cement sinks next to it. My grandma could stay indoors to wash her large family's clothes and bedlinen by hand, rather than lugging it all to a nearby stream and back. Even so, doing the laundry remained a tough, boring, and time-consuming job. Grandma kept an eye on the new labor-saving inventions that industrialization came up with and one day her dream became real: the "magic" washing machine.

My father was Berta's second child—actually, her third-born. Her first child was born in a hospital but the baby died. Pappa finished his six years of schooling at the age of fourteen. He got a job as a bricklayer's apprentice at the local brickworks—nowadays, it would be classed as child labor, and the older men often mistreated the lads. Still, in those days, young men in growing families made a critical contribution to the household income.

For my father, the very worst thing about his job was neither the poor conditions nor the low wages but the fact that he lost it when he was seventeen. For him, being unemployed was utterly shameful, even though it was a fate he shared with many others during the economic crisis of the 1930s. To be useful, he mended the neighbors' shoes.

On the morning of April 9, 1940, the German army invaded Norway and Denmark. My father was called up to fight just a few hours after the news was broadcast. The next day, he was handed a rifle and posted to Landskrona, a harbor town in the straits between Denmark and Sweden. The conscripts were ordered to dig trenches to defend Sweden against the Germans.

My father remained in the army throughout the Second World War and was sent to defend in turn our borders with Denmark, Norway, and Finland. He often spoke of how lucky it was that he was never attacked—during his army years, he hadn't even heard a shot fired in anger.

He urged me to be grateful toward all the countries and their soldiers who had shouldered the heavy burden of fighting and defeating the Nazis and their allies. But he disliked the Soviet system. "We're against both the Nazis and the Communists," Pappa always said. Even early on, I was included in that "we." And he was horrified by the colonizing wars started by European countries, some of which had themselves been so recently occupied by the Germans.

Dad dreaded making a fool of himself in front of educated people. He didn't like the buses because he was unsure about how to get a ticket. He wouldn't browse in bookshops because he wasn't clear about how to approach the till or what would happen once he did. When he did grocery delivery jobs for a while, he was sometimes offered something to eat by upper-class folk. He always said "no, thank you," aware that he lacked proper table manners.

Shopping in the private-enterprise supermarkets was out of the question for him. He only went to the Co-op, the shops owned and run by working-class people like him. The Young Eagles, the scouts club run by the Social Democratic Party's youth section, was the only organization for youngsters run by the party. The working-class movement offered group identity to its members and made my dad and his friends feel safe.

After the war, he held down a few short-term jobs. Then he landed the post as coffee roaster at Lindvalls Kaffe and stayed for almost forty years. In the evenings, he would go down to his carpentry workshop in the cellar. Broken things were mended in my family, not thrown away: when the handle on our first plastic bucket cracked, Pappa made it a new wooden handle.

Pappa, a fit and athletic man, was the best orienteer in Uppsala County. When something interested him he always managed to do it well. He was always ready to join in and his can-do attitude inspired all he undertook. For example, there was the time when my reckless friend Hasse rammed his bicycle into a car and the bike's front wheel got twisted into an eight-shape. All the local children knew that the bicycle belonged to Hasse's mother and they also knew what would happen next: "Hell's bells! Hasse will get a hiding tonight." Hasse was often beaten at home. Quick as a flash, my dad gathered up the boy and the bike, and took both down into the cellar. Pappa set about straightening the front wheel; he pulled it and hammered it until the wheel looked perfect again. He replaced the ripped inner tube and found the right paint to cover the scratches in the lacquer. After an hour and a half, Hasse walked home through our housing estate, pushing a fine-looking bicycle.

My father's family were ordinary working-class people but my mother was born into society's very lowest stratum. It was her mother, Grandma Agnes, who had pulled them out of shaming deprivation and into a respectable life. To outsiders, Agnes might well have seemed like just another old woman in a care home but to us she was a heroine.

When Mum asked her then eighty-eight-year-old mother if there was anything she could do to make her happy, Agnes answered: "Find out who my father was."

Agnes was born in 1891 in Uppsala County. Her tiny first home was on the outskirts of a village. She always said it was no better than a hovel with a dirt floor. Her mother, who was nineteen years old when she had Agnes, never spoke about her daughter's father.

Years later we learned about a tradition that gave an unmarried woman the chance to identify the father of her child by giving her newborn the same name as one of his legitimate children. In Agnes's case, her mother had worked on a farm where the farmer's wife just some months earlier had given birth to a girl named Agnes. The man himself and maybe the local community would have understood.

I was an adult when I asked my grandmother if she had felt deprived during her childhood. Her reply was immediate and definite: "No, I didn't. Not ever. Mum put food on the table every day. We had a roof over our heads, and clean, warm beds to sleep in. We had shoes on our feet and could go to school every day."

All of my grandparents attended school for four years. How much did they learn? I remember how Grandpa Gustav had to spell the words one by one in order to read a newspaper. Neither of my grandmothers could read me stories, and my paternal grandparents could not read aloud to each other from the newspaper.

My parents were literate enough to read novels for pleasure: the generations went through stages of reading ability, from illiteracy to basic reading skills to competence in their own language and, finally, to coping with foreign languages. My grandparents reached, at best, only a basic reading level. My paternal grandfather even advised me against bookishness: reading harmed the eyes, he insisted. He felt like an outsider when his children and grandchildren "buried their noses in books," and preferred carpentry and talking about matters he understood and liked.

One of my questions for Grandma Agnes was why she had married an alcoholic. Hadn't her own foster father taught her enough about living with difficult men?

"I fell in love," she replied unsmilingly. She had found the men in the village unkempt and coarse: "The farm laborers never missed a chance to slap my bottom or touch me in other rude ways," she said. "They would call me all sorts of names because of me being born on the wrong side of the blanket. They knew I would never dare tell my foster father."

Then, one summer, Ville turned up to dig ditches in the parish. Ville's father had been a landless farm laborer but the boy had grown up on the outskirts of Stockholm and served in the army. He helped Agnes carry the milk pails, complimented her hair and always washed at the end of a working day. Ville was not only clean and polite but treated Agnes as a person worthy of respect and not as a bastard child. Such good manners were unheard of in the village. Agnes became pregnant within a month. Ville obeyed the unwritten rule for proper conduct at the time: sex before you marry is acceptable but if you father a child you must marry.

Ville, my maternal grandfather, was an alcoholic who tried to stay sober but lapsed periodically. He was a skilled bricklayer, earned good wages when he wasn't drinking and never beat his wife or his children. Agnes had three children. Her goal in life was to see to it that they had a better life than she had. On two occasions, illness was a serious obstacle to achieving her goal: first, tuberculosis and, later, cancer of the colon. Free universal healthcare came to the rescue. Agnes was cured of tuberculosis and, miraculously, of cancer, too.

Since my mother and her sister were below school age when their mother was in the hospital, they were cared for in a state-funded children's home. During her convalescence female Salvation Army soldiers taught Agnes how to use a sewing machine and she convinced Ville that it would be worth buying one. Making clothes for the children would save money in the long run.

Sewing meant more to her than clothes for her family. It brought her dignity.

My mother's childhood was insecure and unpredictable. She started in primary school in the autumn of 1927. She was enrolled in a fine, newly built school at Vaksala Square, not far from where they lived. Agnes had made her a new dress and held her hand as they walked to school on this very special day. When they arrived at the square and saw the school building, Agnes had to stop to take it all in. Her own school had been a small wooden house and it seemed beyond her wildest imagination that her daughter should be taught inside a school that looked like a fairy-tale castle. She squeezed my mother's hand and whispered: "They must think people like us are worth something because they have built you such a beautiful school."

Inside the school my mother met a teacher who was even more impressive than the building itself. Miss Brunskog was well trained for her job, highly motivated, and keen to use modern teaching methods. She was part of what the state-funded schools could offer to the children from Uppsala's remaining slums, with their still nameless lanes and alleys. These children were not only very well taught but were also, just as importantly, given self-confidence. The teacher arranged for my mother to go to summer camps for children with tubercular parents. She could talk forever about these wonderful summers. *The* high point was when they were taken to see Selma Lagerlöf, who lived at Mårbacka, not far from the camp. Mum remembered how she and her friends sat on the floor and listened as one of the greatest names in Swedish literature read aloud to them from her own books.

At school, my mother caught tuberculosis, the disease that nearly killed her own mother. The state-funded health service looked after her and, while she was recovering at home, the family were given tokens to exchange for free milk from the local corner shop. She told me of how embarrassing it felt to pay with a token, because it signaled to other shoppers that she was from a tubercular family. All Agnes said when she complained was: "Oh dear. But the milk is tasty, don't you think?"

Her mother was satisfied if the family had a good life and material needs were met, one way or the other. Yet my mother wanted more and was frustrated because she lacked what she wanted most of all—a good education. She loved her studies but there was no way she could persuade her father to let her carry on after the end of the six foundation years. It seemed a special injustice when, in her last year at school, a teacher asked her if she wouldn't mind tutoring some of the more well-heeled children in her class. Why should she help them achieve the marks they needed for entry into higher education when she had not been allowed even to apply? So at the age of fifteen, my mother started work as a delivery girl for the local grocer's shop.

My family history over the past century has helped me to understand developments in the wider world. There had been famine years and extreme poverty in my grandmother's recent past, awful conditions that were the main reason why so many of my ancestors migrated to Illinois, Minnesota, and Oregon in 1846 and later. Grandma Agnes and Britta, my mother, were able to make the move from crippling poverty to quite contented lives thanks to many factors coming together and reinforcing each other.

In the first place, Sweden's economic growth explains how my Grandpa Ville, could always find, despite being an intermittent alcoholic, bricklaying work in the construction industry. His wages grew steadily and so he could afford the cost of a sewing machine despite often spending recklessly on booze.

Secondly, there were the state-financed social services, which included not only healthcare and schooling but also children's homes and rehabilitation clinics for alcoholics. Grandpa Ville, for one, would have been worse off still without the treatment he received in one of these clinics. While he was there, he wrote love letters to his wife. We still have one of them, so full of love and deeply passionate pleas for forgiveness. It helps explain why Grandma put up with a married life of constant insecurity.

Thirdly, civil society stepped in at several stages to support and even rescue my marginalized family. Such civic support ranged from the sewing lessons given to Grandma Agnes by the now defunct "slum sisters" of the Salvation Army, to the cultural education my mother, Britta, received from undergraduate volunteers at summer camps. I have come to regard my background as shaped by the combined enterprises set up by the private marketplace, civil society, and the government. My grandmother's and mother's families were lifted out of destitution. Children of my generation benefited from the protection of the welfare state.

True, economic circumstances changed faster than cultural and social norms. Attitudes toward sexuality remained unchanged for an astonishingly long time and the acceptance of sex as an aspect of day-to-day life was utterly taboo. In particular, I'm thinking of access to contraception and also to what we now refer to rather pompously as "sexual and reproductive health and rights." Women in my grandmothers' and mother's generations were not supposed to take pleasure in sexual intimacy and were denied the right to plan when to conceive—outcomes of cultural norms that guided political decisions. Having given birth to three children and barely survived TB and cancer, Grandma Agnes decided that she didn't want any more children. Bringing up the three she had was more than enough responsibility. She had heard about a man who would explain how to use condoms. (Informing the public about condoms—let alone making them available to the public—was expressly forbidden in Swedish law from 1910 to 1938.)

One day in the mid-1920s, Grandma and some of her women friends heard that, someday soon, this brave man would stand in the main square in Uppsala and talk about condoms. They steeled themselves and risked going along to listen to him. The man—the leader of Sweden's most left-wing party at the time—climbed up on a wooden box and gave a straightforward speech about how couples have the right to make up their own minds about when to have a child together. The police arrested him the moment he produced a condom from his jacket pocket to show the gathered crowd.

A decade or so later, in 1935, my mother was fourteen years

old. Her best friend, also fourteen, became pregnant. She lived in an apartment on the same landing as Mamma's family, on the second floor of a tenement block. The girl's pregnancy proved what most people had suspected: her father had been abusing her for a long time. Soon, the entire block knew. The father was interrogated by the police and a few days later the local vicar called to talk with the family. He blamed the mother: it was her fault that her husband had been having sex with their daughter—the mother had obviously not been "available" enough.

This was the reality of life for my mother's generation. She was eighteen years old when she fell in love with my father. Between them, they had no idea about contraception and she became pregnant. She was working full-time doing grocery deliveries while pursuing her dream of higher education by going to evening classes. In other words, the young couple had very little money and my mother did not want to have a child just then. She searched for a way to have an abortion and heard of a doctor with a private surgery. He was also known to reduce his fee for low-income clients.

Mamma went to see the doctor late one afternoon. She was mortified when he requested her to strip and walk around naked in his surgery. When he asked her for sexual services in return for the abortion, she left. Her only other option was to approach someone at work who was known to perform cheap abortions. This woman turned up in my mother's single-room apartment one evening. Her approach to the job was to advance a knitting needle into the womb. During the night that followed, my mother gave birth to a dead fetus and immediately burned it, as instructed, in her small stove. She was lucky to escape the life-threatening hemorrhages or infections that were very common outcomes of these interventions.

Contraception became more widely available following the information breakthrough that accompanied the launch of the National Society for Sexual Information (RFSU) under the leadership of Elise Ottesen-Jensen—who became so famous in Sweden that people knew her by the name "Ottar." It was mainly in response to agitation by her organization that the Swedish parliament legalized both information about and distribution of contraceptives in 1938. To this day, RFSU has remained Sweden's key condom supplier. My mother and my grandmother never missed any opportunity to praise Ottar for her contribution to these life-changing decisions.

When I was in primary school, my father would sometimes take me to the lectures given at the city's branch of the Workers' Educational Association (ABF). The lecture theater was a big space that could hold audiences of many hundreds. The lecturers were often explorers who described their experiences in faraway countries, using a modernized version of a magic lantern, a forerunner of the projector, that displayed enlarged black-and-white photographs on a screen. For me, a young boy, these evenings were truly magical. It was thrilling to go with my pappa to events for grown-ups and I was fascinated by the stories from the colonized countries in distant parts of the world.

The talks were very varied and some of the lecturers were especially impressive. Eric Lundqvist was one of them: he was a game warden who went off to the Dutch East Indies in the 1930s to take up a post offered by the colonial administration that ran what is today Indonesia. Lundqvist married a local woman and later became a well-known writer, admired for his understanding of both the area's natural world and its society. Both my parents read his books and liked his public stance as an anti-racist.

The explorer and speaker Sten Bergman, a biologist with an impressive knowledge of nature in general and birds in particular, was in some ways Lundqvist's direct opposite. In one of his evening lectures, Bergman deviated from the subject of birdwatching in New Guinea to show a short, silent film shot in black-and-white. It featured an odd experiment on the local people: he had made them raise a smooth four-meter-tall pole, which was smeared with soap and had a new, fine-looking axe driven into the top of it. The locals were urged to climb it and we watched their doomed attempts to get the axe. Halfway through, my dad stood, took my hand and said: "Let's leave now." As we walked out of the hall, I saw that my dad's face had gone pale, as it did on the rare occasions when he was angry. He whispered to me: "That man shows no respect. Bergman is a snob. His idea of fun was to trick these people into looking comical just because they wanted the axe. But they are forest dwellers and could use a good axe. I can't stand his attitude."

One evening at the Education Institute, I ran into my classmate Ingmar, whose dad also used to bring his son along to the lectures. Ingmar's dad was a minister in the Swedish Mission Church and had worked as a missionary in French Equatorial Africa. He had once come to our school and given an illustrated talk about this work. I remember it well: the colonized country he described was very different from anything we knew. For all that he was a man of the Church, he spoke most of the time about practical ways of helping the natives—as we called the Congolese people at the time—especially with education and healthcare. When Ingmar was ten, he left school to go with his family for a third tour in the Congo.

For a child of my social class, it was unusual to have such close contact with someone who had traveled to Africa and actually lived there. After Ingmar left, my teacher picked me once to post a letter to him from everyone in the class. I can still recall the excitement I felt at sending my first ever airmail letter. The address of the boarding school for the missionaries' children read strangely and I learned for the first time the name of an African city—Pointe-Noire, now the most important port in the Republic of the Congo.

I was taught a lot of geography at school but in the end was left with the feeling that I knew amazingly little about how people lived in other parts of the world. Generally speaking, school instilled a worldview based on a vague notion of "the West" against "the Rest." "The Rest" was where "the natives" lived and, apparently, their cultures were pretty primitive.

My teacher in, I think, year five (we were twelve years old then) once memorably insisted that Hinduism made people in India fatalistic, so persuading them to convert to Christianity was very important for their country's progress and development. No one taught me anything about India's ancient civilizations. Long before the Swedes had got round to carving a handful of signs into rune stones, Indians were writing in their own alphabets.

Did the Soviet Union, Japan, and the South American countries belong to the West or not? We were never told. The progress of colonized nations toward independence was something I heard about at home from my father rather than from my teachers at school. Overall, my mental outlook was shaped at home, influenced by my relatives and especially my mother and father, and the radio broadcasts we listened to. School played a very minor role.

Mum was cured of her TB. Sweden's economy, and my father's wages, improved faster than my parents could ever have hoped for. I was only five years old when we moved into a house with a nice garden with plenty of fruit trees. To my parents, the house was a dream come true. They were able to buy it mainly through years of saving, topped up by a loan guaranteed by the state through the growing social housing movement. It was an initiative aimed at stimulating home ownership for the working class. They also had to take on a private bank loan and a generous loan offered by my unmarried uncle, Martin.

The house was new and modern: it had central heating, running hot and cold water, a bathroom with an enameled tub, and a kitchen with an electric cooker, a fridge, and a washing machine. The local library was nearby, just down the street. Mum regularly walked with me to borrow books that she would read to me. Other families with children lived in the neighboring houses and I soon got friendly with some of them.

My father used to like to show me the massive cables from the generating station at Bergeforsen and explain how the hydro power was transformed into electric current for our washing machine. One of his favorite enterprises was to go around picking up large pine branches from forest clearings near the city. His employers let him have weekend use of a company car so he could transport the branches home to become fuel for our central heating and water boiler.

My parents' garden was largely devoted to useful plants: they grew potatoes, various vegetables, apples and strawberries. Mum sewed almost all our clothes because buying ready-made was expensive, with one exception: underpants. I remember when imported underwear was first in the shops, and how my mum would chat over the hedge with our neighbors about the pros and cons of foreign undies: what if wearing them was bad for children's health? This early, embryonic sign of global trading in consumer goods—underpants from Portugal—was instantly seen as deeply suspect.

Our saving and skimping meant that, after a few years in our new house, we could go on family holidays. My parents bought a red moped and a blue tandem bicycle, and Mum actually sewed a tent for us. The first time, we toured Uppsala County and were never farther than about a hundred kilometers from our house. We ended up visiting Grandma Agnes's two unmarried brothers, who lived together on the family farm and welcomed us warmly.

I was allowed to ride bareback on their large horse, led by Petrus, the older brother. When my dad photographed me on the horse, it highlighted a clash of cultures. Pappa thought one snap was especially successful: the massive farm horse with the city boy on its back, next to the old farmer in his tall boots.

Hans as a child on a horse

He sent a copy of the photograph to Petrus as a gesture of appreciation for the hospitality we had been shown. It was not well received. Petrus was offended because the photo showed him in his overalls and boots. If he was to be photographed it would only be when he wore his single dark suit. If city folk took photos of him in his working clothes, they presumably intended to make fun of their country-bumpkin relative. My parents eventually settled the conflict but it took them the best part of two years. It was a reminder always to respect cultural differences. Petrus was a wise, kind man and that made the lesson all the more effective.

We took the moped on our second holiday and traveled as far as Copenhagen. My brother, Mats, was born in 1960, when I was twelve years old. Three years later, the family invested in a gray VW Beetle and we went on holiday to Norway. Then in 1972, my parents took another big step by buying a piece of land by the sea. My dad built a holiday cottage on the site. He used the money he had inherited from his mother to buy a small boat with an outboard engine and gave it her name—Berta.

Having been a housewife for over a decade, my mother got a part-time job in a library in nearby Old Uppsala. She also went to adult education college every evening to get secondary-school competence in Swedish, English, and Social Studies—but she never got the real education she always dreamed of, which would have allowed her to become a teacher or a journalist.

The story of my family was mirrored countrywide by so many others and demonstrated exceptionally fast and positive changes in all aspects of life in Sweden. To get from my grandma's four years of basic schooling to my professorial chair took just three generations. To give an example of an even more dramatic change: four generations ago, my great-grandmother was illiterate. As a family, we reflect the different levels of education in today's world.

It is easy to see the four economical levels in the world exemplified in the context of my family. Improved healthcare allowed people to escape the burden of infectious disease and to lead longer, healthier lives. Rising material welfare meant that it took only a couple of generations to move from shacks with dirt floors to spacious modern houses. Yet none of this would have seemed straightforward to the individuals themselves who, step by step, achieved life-changing personal advances.

2

Discovering the World

I had always been curious about the world, so I saved up money to go traveling. When I was sixteen, I embarked, on my own, on a cycling trip that took me around England and Wales. I remember, when I stopped to look around the first village on my route, seeing a stone column inscribed with names: a list of all the villagers who had died in the First World War, almost twenty names from such a small community. As I walked around the lovingly looked-after monument, I saw another list of names, almost as long, of those who had died in the Second World War.

Faced with my first British war memorial, I assumed the village must have suffered exceptional losses. But over the next six weeks, as I cycled though Wales, Somerset, Devon, and along the south coast back to London, I saw similar war memorials in almost every town and village. And in conversations with other young people I met on my trip, I learned that often one or both of their parents had been killed or injured during the war.

I finally began to grasp what my dad had tried to tell me about these huge, recent wars; their cruelty as well as their extent and how differently countries in Europe had been affected. Growing up in Sweden had made it difficult for me to fully take on board twentieth-century European history.

In the summer of 1966, aged eighteen, I hitchhiked to Paris, then down to the Riviera and farther south to Rome. From the heel of Italy I went by boat to Greece. The Greek countryside was unlike anything I had ever seen before. Many family homes looked like very basic shelters. Old ladies, with covered heads and dressed in black, walked along the road carrying huge loads of wood on their backs. Traveling back to Sweden through Macedonia, Montenegro, Croatia, Slovenia, Austria, and Germany was a journey of gradually improving conditions.

My way home went via Berlin. At the time, the Berlin Wall had been in place for five years. I crossed the border at Checkpoint Charlie and spent the whole day walking around East Berlin. It was an effective vaccination against extreme left-wing views: one brief visit to the GDR made it easy to detest communism.

In 1968 Agneta and I traveled south together. Stage one took us to one of Stockholm's southernmost metro stations. We had agreed we would start hitchhiking from there. And just at that spot, outside a big office block, we had our first quarrel.

The slip road to the southbound motorway was just a short stretch away so, obviously, I wanted to get on with it. Agneta gestured at the sun, which was nearing the top of its course across the sky and said that it was lunchtime—we should have something to eat. We stared doubtfully at each other.

"Let's snack on something while we try to get a car to stop," I said.

"Hundreds of cars pass by here every minute," Agneta pointed out. "We have all summer ahead of us. Look over there, a seat in the shade and a nice view into the park. Come on, we should eat the food I packed now. It's in your bag."

I don't mind skipping meals but on the first day of our first joint holiday, she made it very clear that I ought to change my bad habits. We had an enjoyable, romantic picnic in the park. The rest of the day went well, too: we hitchhiked all the way to the south of Sweden and stopped at a charming hostel where we, a couple of nineteen-year-olds, took a family room for the night. It meant that we could be alone together without other backpackers turning up to join us.

Agneta was already in bed when I came out after my shower.

"Our toothbrushes are in the toiletries bag on the edge of the basin," she told me.

I located the gear and started brushing. Odd-tasting tooth-paste, I thought, but I couldn't take my eyes off the love of my life, who was watching me smilingly from the bed. Such a very warm smile. Then she began to giggle and, after a few seconds, burst out laughing. I didn't get it. It unnerves a romantic youth wearing only a towel when his girlfriend laughs at him. Agneta was still laughing when my field of vision filled with white foam bubbling out of my mouth. She came over to help me. I had been brushing my teeth with shampoo.

We traveled far that summer, first by ferry across the Baltic Sea to Poland then onward through Eastern Europe to Istanbul. We took more or less the same route back home.

By the time I left school, ready for university, I had traveled through most of Europe, east and west. Now, my obsession with understanding the world had moved on to the greater part, which was outside Europe. It was a major change.

I grew up during the Cold War and to my generation the future depended on whether a nuclear war between East and West could be avoided. In 1968, the Soviet Union occupied Czechoslovakia and crushed the "Prague Spring," a series of liberalizing reforms by that country's government. It was a big set-back but there were also some inspiring aspects to this episode. It suggested that communism might well begin to crumble internally.

My generation had become intensely aware of the need for better living conditions almost everywhere in the world. I had heard the missionary father of my third-year classmate list the fundamental things that needed improving: education, healthcare, roads and jobs. The world at large had not benefited from the kinds of social changes that had meant so much to my family and our wider circle of relatives.

It baffled me that the West supported so many regimes with little interest in useful reforms, while poor, communist countries such as Cuba, Vietnam, and China were actually on the move, making better decisions, and showing unmistakable signs of social advances. It was truly confusing—but I never joined the wave of extreme left-wing protest either in 1968 or later. I felt antipathy toward communism, and social democracy gave me a deep-rooted sense of belonging.

When I started university, the dominant conflict was still the Vietnam War. By this time, the Vietnamese regime that the US army was propping up seemed to have no prospects of survival. During my final years at the Cathedral School in Uppsala, I had initially been alone in my opposition to America's role in Vietnam. But at university, my interest in politics dwindled just as it was increasing among most of the other students.

I have always disliked the romanticizing of revolutions and glorifying of armed conflict. People who are keen on politics tend to overrate the impact of political reforms. In fact, effective reform of living conditions is rarely due to policies and mostly to changes in the conditions for development. The man who guided me to think along those lines was a Mozambican scientist working in the USA. I met him for the first time in the autumn of 1967.

In 1960s Sweden, it was common to have grown up in a simple home and for your father to work in a factory. But to be the first in your family to go to university was rare and special. Now, a few weeks into my first year as a student, I felt that joining the Social Democrats was allowing me to fulfill an unspoken expectation of my parents back home.

The small student society had made me its international secretary and given me a task straightaway: to organize an evening session for our group to meet a man called Eduardo Mondlane.

Mondlane had been born and grew up in Mozambique. He was one of the first Black students from his home country to be sponsored to attend an American university. The USA offered plenty of opportunities for talented people and Mondlane had eventually become an associate professor at Syracuse University in New York. Later, he had left his academic career behind and returned to Africa, where he led FRELIMO, the Mozambican Liberation Front, headquartered in recently independent Tanzania. In 1964, FRELIMO had crossed the border and begun an armed insurrection against the Portuguese government.

Eduardo Mondlane had now come to Sweden on a mission to raise Swedish support for the independence fighters. I was very embarrassed that only eight students had turned up to listen to him. When his taxi stopped outside, I was expecting an African Che Guevara. But instead of a bearded guerrilla in camouflage kit and boots, the man who emerged from the car was a clean-shaven gentleman in a sober gray suit and well-polished shoes. He put me at ease when I apologized for the small audience, and the moment he was inside suggested that we should sit on the sofas around the coffee table in the corner.

His outward appearance was reserved and ordinary, but what he had to tell us was mind-blowing. It is no exaggeration to say that the well-argued case he presented during the next two hours would prove decisive for my entire professional life to come.

In summary, this is what he said: "We, the black Mozambicans, have no quarrel with the white race in general, nor with the Portuguese language and culture. We confine our struggle to gaining independence for our country from the colonial rulers sent by the fascist regime in Lisbon. War is terrible but we are forced to fight for our freedom. I believe the outcome will be not only liberation of our own country but also freeing Portugal of fascism."

What followed was still more thought-provoking: "Actually, becoming independent is the easy part. We will win our liberation war because the Portuguese soldiers think dying in defense of fascism and colonialism is an undignified death. Winning the war is one thing but the harder task facing us Mozambicans is to improve living conditions for the people. Their expectations will be so high and our capacity to meet them will be so limited."

He was referring to the difficulties experienced by most of the recently independent African countries. His conclusion was that

Mozambique, with its very high incidence of illiteracy and near-total lack of highly educated people, would find dealing with the problems of development even more challenging than these other countries. It impressed me tremendously to hear a commander of a war discuss postwar challenges.

Before he left, he said farewell to each one of us personally.

"What are you studying? And when are your final exams?" he asked me.

I was nineteen, a first-year undergraduate taking a course in statistics before starting my medical training. The thought of finals had not yet entered my head. I probably stuttered as I said: "My medical studies are due to start next term and I'll qualify . . . as a doctor in . . . 1975."

"Excellent. By then, Mozambique should be an independent state. Promise you'll come to work with us as a doctor. We will need you," Mondlane said and smiled. Then our eyes met, his face went serious and, as we shook hands, I heard myself say: "Yes. I promise."

Two years later, on February 3, 1969, Eduardo Mondlane was murdered by a targeted explosion in Dar es Salaam, the capital of Tanzania. I was reminded of my promise but knew that this loss made it more likely that the Mozambican liberation struggle would fail.

Eduardo Mondlane had helped us to understand the tragedy of having to go to war to achieve independence, and that his war was waged against the colonizing state and not against the people who had come to colonize his country. What he said stayed with me. I would later hear Nelson Mandela speak in the same spirit. It took another ten years before I was able to take up a medical post in Mozambique, and it took me a lifetime to fully understand Mondlane's central message: becoming independent is relatively easy. What is more difficult is to develop a country suffering from the illiteracy, disease, and extreme poverty left in the wake of generations of colonial rule.

* * *

I was elected to the International Committee of the Uppsala Student Union early on in my medical studies.

One day, the secretary maneuvered me into the corridor and whispered in my ear: "Never ask that question again." During the meeting that had just concluded in the room next door, I had raised a concern about the budget. The accounts included a vaguely described investment in a trust that had inexplicably lost a great deal of money.

Now the secretary explained the secrecy: "the trust" was money set aside to offer short-term loans to students who needed to travel to Poland for an abortion. The sum had shrunk because last autumn more women than usual had made the trip and many had not yet saved up enough to repay the loan. I had heard about Catholic Poland's abortion services and naturally promised to ask no more questions, and to not reveal to anyone what he had told me.

It was only in 1975 that Sweden legalized abortion. Remarkably, that was three years after similar legislation had been passed in India. I learned a great deal more about matters such as this on my study trip to India in 1972: in 1970, since Agneta and I were both growing more intent on satisfying our curiosity about the world, we started planning our great trip to Asia.

My parents did not approve when I told them about our plan. One reason was probably that I would have to take six months off my medical studies. They were upset at the notion that such a fine education be put on hold. Still, their main argument was that the journey might be dangerous, even though they realized and accepted that they had no control over what we did. As my mother said by way of ending the discussion: "For your dad and me, higher education was just a dream. Now, we no longer understand you. You have educated yourself away from us."

The War of Independence in Bangladesh broke out in the spring of 1971 and continued almost until the end of that year. The war affected me directly. Agneta and I had by then made detailed plans for our travels. The basic idea had been to drive in a VW camper van along Indian country roads but the war meant that the India–Pakistan border was closed. We had to rethink.

Toward the end of the year, Agneta completed her nursing exams and started her first job. I had finished my fourth year as a medical student and could take up locum posts. We had saved up the money we needed and set out on February 8, 1972.

The word "backpacking" had not yet entered the language but we did check in two very full rucksacks on the flight to Sri Lanka. The package trip included two weeks in a pretty little beach hotel that we really enjoyed. However, our reserved seats on the return charter flight to Sweden were empty. Instead we traveled on, first around the island and then to India by the regular ferry service. When we arrived at Rameswaram in India, we had to go down a short flight of steps and jump into a rowing boat to reach the beach. The customs and border officials were housed in tents. Assisted by barefoot soldiers in khaki shorts and knee-high woolen legwarmers, they kept an eye on us travelers. The soldiers were armed with impressive, old-style rifles. The entry protocol was exceptionally careful. Blood samples were collected and checked to exclude malaria infection. Our yellow World Health Organization cards were examined to make sure that we had been vaccinated against smallpox. Down there on the beach, the Indian state functioned very well.

During our month in Sri Lanka, we had been amazed by the country's ancient history. It was news to us that the written form of Sinhalese, the language of the largest population group, had been in use for more than two thousand years. Equally humbling was the sight of the several-thousand-year-old water reservoirs and irrigation systems. They were proof not only of impressive engineering skills in the very distant past but also of how ignorant we were. We had not had the faintest idea that the Sri Lankan civilization had been so advanced.

Our sense of shame deepened in India. During our first few days, we visited ancient temples and realized that all the different languages of India had alphabets which had been in use for many thousands of years. This was so different from my travels in Greece. There, I had already been aware of great landmarks and historical events. It was intellectually painful to be a tourist in Sri Lanka and India. And it would get worse yet.

Part of the plan for our Asian trip was for me to be a visiting student at the St. John's Medical College in Bangalore. That "elective" period of study completely changed my views about India. The course was good but the effect on me was due less to the content and more to the first hours of teaching on the first day. I gained a brutal insight: the Indian fourth-year medical students knew much more than I did. I had definitely been a keen student, perhaps not always top of the class but usually with marks in the upper range. I admit I arrived in India convinced that I, a high-flying Swedish medical student, would outclass the locals. But, once there, it became instantly obvious that in India I was near the bottom of the class.

On my first day, I was asked to join a group of students for an instructive run-through of yesterday's X-rays from the medical ward. The first film was a so-called angiogram—an image of contrast-injected blood vessels in a particular organ. This one showed the blood vessels in the kidney. The investigation had been made because the patient had presented with blood in his urine.

I remember my feeling of shock that an Indian hospital was able to do angiograms. In this case, the procedure involved inserting a thin, flexible plastic tube—a catheter—into the large artery in the groin and advancing it up into the aorta. Once the tip of the catheter reached the aortic branch that supplied arterial blood to the kidney, the radiologist injected the contrast liquid. The X-rays of the injected kidney would then show its blood vessels.

The procedure had been distinctly dangerous until 1953, when the Swedish clinician Sven Ivar Seldinger, researching the method at the Karolinska Institute, came up with the idea of the long plastic catheter. It made the investigation easier and safer. My Swedish clinical teachers used to boast about this advancement and point out that it made the technique more widely used internationally. Even so, in 1972, I arrogantly believed that an Indian university hospital surely wouldn't be ready to handle it.

I stared at the beautiful pattern of branching blood vessels on the screen in front of us. The image quality was as good as anything I had seen in my Swedish university hospital. While I pondered the amazingly high standard of care in the Indian hospital, I suddenly realized that the blood vessels in the upper part of the kidney looked unusual—thinner than normal and clustered into a ball shape. It surely signified a tumor, possibly cancerous.

The Indian doctor asked the group: "Why would this patient pass blood in their urine?"

It would be polite, I told myself, to let the Indian students have a go before I told them what was what. In retrospect, I recognize of course that this was just another symptom of my superiority fantasy.

"The reason there's blood in the patient's urine must be the tumor we can see here in the upper part of the kidney," said the first Indian student to answer. "The patient is lucky because it's a relatively small tumor and discovered early. When we examined him, it was actually impossible to palpate it through the abdominal wall. And he said the pressure didn't cause him any pain."

The radiologist asked why it was that the cancer had been detected so early. Another student, who had also been on the ward when the history was taken, said that the patient had gone to the doctor immediately on finding blood in his urine. Unlike many, he hadn't tried out folk medicine first. The student added that this was likely to be at least partly because the patient trusted modern medicine, given that he was an electrical engineer employed by a local telephone manufacturer.

One after the other, the students answered the follow-up questions concerning other possible early symptoms of kidney cancer. I stopped trying to answer the instructor's questions and instead tried to work out how the others knew so much more than me.

Walking out into the corridor afterward, I turned to some of the other students and asked why I had ended up in a training session for specialists. I added by way of explanation that I should really have been with the fourth-year students.

"We're all fourth-years," they said. "What's the problem?"

I told them how impressed I had been by their knowledge about all the likely symptoms of kidney cancer and also about other illnesses that had been discussed.

"Which textbook do you use?" I asked.

"Most of us go for Harrison," one of them said.

Harrison is the abbreviated name of the biggest existing textbook in clinical medicine: at the time, 1,120 tightly printed pages. I was an ambitious student, and had bought this tome the year before, in 1971. Still unread many years later, it sits on the bookshelf behind me as I write this sentence. To pass the Swedish exams, I mugged up using a condensed manual with bigger print and half as many pages. As we carried on comparing medical studies in Sweden and India, it became obvious that Indian students spent much more time re-reading their big books than their Swedish colleagues devoted to their brief handbooks. The world view that I had grown up to accept unthinkingly—that West was best and the rest would never catch up—had for the first time been challenged and changed.

We had expected to encounter poverty in India and we certainly did. But we had been ignorant of the region's great, ancient civilizations and also of how advanced the talented young Indians were in the areas of modern academic learning and skills.

* * *

We continued our journey from Bangalore. The Indian train company offered students low-priced third-class tickets and we spent many hours on trains. We passed the time talking and it made us realize the diversity of this huge country. In Nepal, we changed to bus travel and, once in the capital, Kathmandu, we set out on foot, hiking for four days along the paths of Himalayan valleys.

Thanks to a government trekking permit, we were able to find cheap places to sleep along the route, in family homes where we were given lentils and rice to eat. These kind, proud people scraped a meager living from growing maize on the terraced slopes. The communities looked well organized but conditions were tough. There were few schools and healthcare was nonexistent. The women bore an average of six children, of whom one or two usually died: infant mortality was 25 percent. It was also common for girls to be married off in their early teens.

After several hours of trudging uphill with the snow-clad peaks of Mount Everest in sight, we crossed the trail itself. We crossed an alarming suspension bridge and then climbed a final steep hillside. We were exhausted by then and sat down on the ground at a Buddhist place of prayer. A little girl came walking along, saw us and made a "sleep" gesture, leaning her cheek against her hands. She took us home to meet her parents, who gave us their bedroom in the upper floor of their straw-roofed two-story house.

There was a full moon that night. The village people gathered to play and sing in the moonlight but our host family did not join the others. They chose to stay at home to bathe their not-quite-year-old baby. The little boy was washed in a basin of warm water, dried and rubbed with butter and then given ground cereal mush to eat. All this was done by the couple working together. They did not mind us watching them from where we lay in bed just a few meters away. Agneta—a nurse—started making de-

Nepalese suspension bridge

tailed notes in her diary. Her description of what they did soon grew into several pages of text. Around us, the valley air was clear and resonated with the tremendous organ roar of the mountain streams rushing past the village.

The next day, the family's great-grandmother took us for a walk to the fields to show us how they cultivated them. We took photos, feeling we had gained real insight into their way of life.

Just in case we should ever return, we made a note of their names. And in 2014, forty-two years later, we did return. By then, the track to the village was fit for cars to travel all the way. Men in hi-viz vests with the transport authority logo shoveled sand to stabilize the road and clear the ditches. Fish farms had started up for export production. Schools had multiplied, infant mortality decreased and family size was approaching an average of two children.

But we recognized where we were when we arrived at the home of our old hosts. The house still stood, but in modernized form. Tin had replaced straw as a roof covering, just as in the other houses in the valley. The baby we had watched being washed now lived in the house with his own family: his mother had died twenty years earlier but his wife was as hospitable as his mother had been. His elderly father had gone to live in India. We had brought with us photographs from our first visit and showed them to friends and relatives from their neighborhood.

During the meal, we were told that all the local children were vaccinated now and they all went to school. Family planning was much better and the village health center offered the morning-after pill. Infant mortality was now only 4 percent. However, there were still problems—many of the girls left for the city to work as sex workers.

It rained that night but instead of leaving a sour, stale smell behind as had been the case during our last visit, the water poured off the tin roof. "Still, the straw roofs were surely prettier? Do you really prefer tin?" I asked the villagers. One of the men stepped closer to me.

"Listen, a tin roof lasts for twenty years. No maintenance for twenty years! We had to renew the straw roofs every second year: every two years we had to go out to cut the grass, take it home and dry it."

"And now the house is dry inside and that stale smell is gone," many of the women insisted.

I stood looking at the tin roofs for a while. The move from straw roofs and teenage brides to decent living conditions can often involve very ugly periods of transition—prostitution, slums, exploitation. And tin roofs. But simultaneously the forces of progress are at work, creating economic growth, better health and education, smaller families and increased individual rights. As you observe societies in transition, it is easy to focus on the ugliness. But the people I spoke to in Nepal knew where they were going and they were happy to be on the journey.

Before we left the village after this second visit, Agneta opened her old diary and read aloud the story of how the young parents had washed and fed their baby one night in 1972. Everyone was moved. The grown man who was once that baby wept. We wept, too, and gave him a photo of his mother. He put it away in a box kept for important papers and mementos. It was his only photo of her.

Back in 1972, we traveled southeast from the mountain villages of Nepal, first back to India, and then on to Burma (now Myanmar), Thailand, Malaysia, and Singapore. We ended our grand tour with a month in Indonesia.

Our Asian adventure had lasted for six wonderful months and we had learned a lot. Better still, we had made a significant decision: back home, the first thing we did was get married. We agreed that a full-on wedding ceremony would feel awkward since we had lived together for so many years already. Besides, we had

Four photographs of the Nepalese family,
two from 1972 and two from 2014

spent all our savings. Instead, our marriage was registered at City Hall where the presiding judge read a poem that made us both burst into tears of happiness. We shared a peach in the park afterward and then picked up our bikes to ride to my parents' home and tell them we were properly married now. My dad was delighted that he hadn't been forced to face a formal wedding but my mum never forgave us for ruining her chance to throw a party. Agneta's parents learned the news from a postcard sent to their summer holiday house in southern Sweden. They phoned to congratulate us.

An important event took place on April 25, 1974: Portugal's fascist regime fell. A couple of days earlier we had brought our first child home from the maternity hospital.

We lived near the hospital. That morning, we strolled home through the city park, pushing baby Anna in her pram. It had been a trouble-free birth and our daughter was in excellent shape. The delicate blue squills that always told us spring was here were flowering in the brilliant sunshine and we loved watching Anna sleep peacefully.

At one point that afternoon, I sneaked away to listen to the news and heard of the successful, bloodless coup in Portugal. Later, Agneta and I listened together to the evening news roundup and got the impression that the takeover of power had been expected. What Eduardo Mondlane had once predicted with such certainty had actually happened. And it seemed to me, remembering my promise to Eduardo, that one happy young family—mine—would soon be able to set to work in a soon-to-be-independent Mozambique.

After our trip to Asia, and throughout my final eighteen months of medical training, my obsession with the world had grown more practical. Agneta and I had decided we would work for a few years in one of the poorest countries in Africa. Agneta had applied to join a training course in midwifery as a useful addition to her nursing skills and we had begun to plan in earnest for living and working in Africa as a family.

During Agneta's pregnancy, we had agreed that I should be at home with the baby from October. Agneta took the idea of shared parenthood very seriously and was planning to complete her midwifery training during that autumn of 1974. As October came around, I was working at the Uppsala pulmonary medicine clinic as a locum and was hoping for a permanent post there for when I returned from Mozambique.

I kept hanging back from speaking to the head of the clinic but one day I knew this could not be postponed any longer. I explained that my wife had to finish her training in the autumn, and I wanted to take time off, from October to February.

"Time off? But you're the locum. I can't hire a locum for the locum," he said.

"I see but . . . is there no chance that you could do precisely that?"

"If you leave now you can always come back in February if there's a job up for grabs. But you have to stay on if you want to keep the post you're in."

"But next year they'll legislate for rights to paternal leave," I said.

"Maybe the law will pass, maybe not," the boss said.

I shuffled away and didn't say anything about it over supper. Afterward, when we were sitting on the sofa together, I mentioned having seen the head of the clinic.

"Oh, that's good," Agneta said.

"Yes, well. But if I go on leave I won't be allowed to keep the job," I explained.

"But you seem to land locum posts easily."

"Yes, perhaps, but I thought it might be best if I carry on working this autumn after all."

She just looked at me.

"If you stay at home this autumn," I went on, "I'll have an extra qualification. It will be helpful when I apply for junior doctor posts."

"But what about me completing my training?" Agneta said.

"Perhaps you could do that next year?"

At that point, she got up and went to the wardrobe in our bedroom. She came back a little later, carrying our small suitcase into the hall. She put it down by the front door.

"There you are," she said in a firm but calm tone. Agneta never raised her voice.

"What's that for?" I asked, feeling confused.

"I've packed some things for you, like underwear and socks and shirts. You can get out of my life right now. Don't come back. We agreed about the parental leave and I have notified the course organizers."

The following day, I went to see the head of the clinic again and said I wanted to resign effective from the last day of September. I stayed at home with Anna, as arranged. My wife had placed a packed case by the front door and told me to get out of her life. Regrettably, I admit that this was what it took to make me realize that I really wanted to be at home with my first child.

During these years after Anna's birth, the Swedish anti-apartheid movement responded to requests from African state bodies, including the Ministry of Health in Mozambique, and set up a recruitment center. Its acronym was ARO, which stood for the Africa Recruitment Organization. I was a very active participant in its creation. It took another four years, from the morning when a bloodless military coup ended Portugal's colonial war, before Agneta and I were ready to work in an independent Mozambique.

In November 1975 our son, Ola, was born, while we were living in the northern city of Hudiksvall. Agneta had a job as a midwife and I as a foundation year doctor. We both felt that working in a small Swedish hospital would be a perfect part of our preparations for Mozambique.

These preparations had been intensive. We had taken a year-long combination of courses on topics like risk management and aid organization work in a specialized school at Sandö, some four hundred kilometers north of Stockholm. We had learned to speak Portuguese, arguably one of the most important steps. Another seriously important course, which had taken ten weeks to complete, was the Uppsala-based training in healthcare management in poor countries. To round all this off, we had attended a two-week seminar run by the ARO. After that we were ready to sign the contract. The relevant authorities approved us and the Mozambican health service employed me straightaway. By then, I had begun my specialist training as a physician and both of us had a good three years' experience working as, respectively, a doctor and a midwife. We received our plane tickets, scheduled for August 1978.

We were ready. Then we were abruptly, brutally stopped in our tracks.

In May 1978, I made an alarming discovery when taking a shower late one evening.

"Hans, I'm sorry to have to say this. But . . . yes, the tumor is malignant."

Lasse Wickström, consultant surgeon and head of the department, gave me the verdict later that month. He had asked me to come and see him in his office and his face was serious as he offered me a seat.

The pathology test results had been printed on a piece of yellow paper. He pulled it out from under a desk pad made of green rubber. While Lasse Wickström waited for my reaction before going on to discuss what would happen next, I had time to observe that the shade of green didn't go at all well with the light wood of the desk.

Perhaps ten days had passed since I had made my discovery in the shower. I had been busy soaping my body when my hand stopped and my mind went blank. My fingertips went back to the surface of my right testicle. Yes, a small lump. It was deep under the scrotal skin so it must be on the testicle itself. I compared sides. The left one was smooth. The quick realization grew overwhelming and terrifying. It was almost certainly some form of testicular cancer.

I was alone at home with the children—Anna was four and Ola two years old—while Agneta was on a two-week Portuguese course. By then, we had been granted leave from our Swedish jobs and replacements had been employed. We had signed a contract with a tenant who would rent our apartment for two years and the flights to Mozambique were booked for August. Now it was May. And I had an illness that might kill me in a few years' time.

Luckily, the children were asleep when I made the discovery. I can't tell you how I spent that night because I don't remember.

I do remember how Lasse Wickström examined me the next morning after the ward round.

"Look, because you are going to Mozambique, I need to be 100 percent certain. I'll have a closer look and see what can be done," Lasse had said, and he asked a nurse to book a theater. He scheduled a time for two days later. I decided to keep it to myself and told Agneta that I'd be fine, and she mustn't leave the course early. On the day of the operation, I took the children to nursery as usual.

When I opened my eyes after the surgery, Lasse was leaning over me. He looked serious.

"Can you hear me, Hans?" I nodded. "It wasn't possible to cut the lump out," he said. "Most of it was inside the gland so I removed the whole right testicle. It has been sent to pathology and I'll call you the moment we have the answer."

Walking was painful afterward but apart from that, the days passed as usual. Agneta carried on with her language course. I took the children to nursery in the morning and worked during the day in the department of internal medicine.

And now I sat in Lasse's office, confronting this newly con-firmed knowledge.

"Listen carefully to me now," Lasse said. "It is a seminoma, the nicer kind of testicular cancer. It responds well to radia-tion therapy, so you have a good chance of being cured even if it has spread a little. I've had a word with the radiologists in Uppsala. They will look after you, do some more tests. The radi-ation therapy can start next week. I've fixed you up with three months' sick leave. But you will have to postpone the journey to Mozambique."

Lasse Wickström was a truly kind, thoughtful man. He had already called my department and made things easier for me. I walked from the surgery outpatients to the internal medicine clinic—all of 130 meters—and had a chat with my colleague Per, who was not with a patient just then. He asked me about the outcome of the op, took it on board and discreetly adjusted my fully booked timetable for the afternoon. My colleagues shared the appointments between them. I left because I wanted to collect the children from nursery.

I didn't cry when I made the children's supper, or when we were playing with building blocks on the floor. We were together in the here and now. I read and sang to them as usual.

I finally broke down when Agneta came home that evening. She spoke to the children and invented a story about how I had been working very hard and needed to be left in peace. They were too young to grasp what was going on anyway and were simply pleased that Daddy was home early and had played with them. And Mummy had come home early, too. It made their day.

But then, we did not really grasp what was happening either. Had I received a death sentence? I was a twenty-nine-year-old man, father of two children. I had cancer.

Would I see the children grow up? Would I survive? Agneta and

I hugged and cried together. My mind was filled with the darkest chaos and the strongest love.

When your entire life has changed, you need a plan. What happens next—right now? Tomorrow? Agneta dealt with everything. She thought things through, solved problems and carried me through the days, weeks, and months.

It took her just an hour to arrange three months' unpaid leave from her job. She decided that we would move to her aunt Eda's farm, near Uppsala. She explained this to the children as an alternative to going to Africa, which made sense to them because we used to celebrate Christmas at Aunt Eda's. We packed up the car together. My job was to be with the children and pack their toys. Agneta had only just got her driver's license and was not particularly keen on driving us to Uppsala but she did it all the same.

We arrived on a Sunday. As we approached Uppsala, I was touched to see the castle and the cathedral towers of the place where I had grown up. Suddenly, I felt very sad. Agneta stopped the car so I could go outside and calm down.

The tests and the radiation therapy started the following week. It was hell. It was likely there were cancer cells in the local lymph nodes and there was a suspicion that it had spread to the liver, because some of my liver test values were abnormal. The radiotherapy could deal with any infiltrated lymph nodes. Liver metastases would kill me within the year.

My whole life stopped. Mozambique no longer existed. Survival was all that mattered.

I wept for days while Agneta looked after the children and comforted me. The illness made me want to hurt people around me. They cheerfully carried on with their lives while I was burdened by grief, by misery. All I could be bothered to do was lie on the hammock in the garden and read Inspector Maigret books—all of them. My mother could not bear being around me. She was too grief-stricken to be any kind of support.

On the other hand, Eda and her husband Per pretended that I wasn't ill and that was very restful. They didn't ask me how I felt and concentrated on being helpful in practical ways. Per, who was the deputy harbormaster in the Sigtuna marina, found a small sailing boat for us. Their house was large and we had two rooms to ourselves on the upper floor. It was easy for me to travel from the farm to my treatment sessions in the Uppsala oncology department.

I decided my goal was to live long enough to see the children start school.

A few days of this new existence had passed when something struck me. I was sitting on my bed on the second floor of Eda's farmhouse, looking out over the apple trees, when I suddenly remembered an important fact. Ten years ago, a doctor had spoken to me about my elevated liver values and advised me to stop drinking so much alcohol. Which was irrelevant, because I was teetotal. It should have been followed up but wasn't.

My notes, I thought, should still be in the infectious diseases unit where I had been working at the time. I knew the charge nurse, who was very efficient. In less than a minute, I decided what I must do: speak to the nurse about locating the old records and find out exactly what the lab results had been.

I never give up if there is something I want to know. It's why many people find me unbearable to be around. This trait was obvious even in my teenage self. When I was hitchhiking in Europe, I once stayed in a youth hostel in Marseille. I was the youngest of the backpackers and would go to sit on my own outside, studying my copy of the Swedish Automobile Association's informative *Atlas of Europe*. The others began to call me "the boy with the blue book." Half the atlas comprised a collection of facts about European towns and cities. I memorized a lot and could verify what people said in general conversation, making helpful comments such as: "No, you're wrong, Prague is much older than that."

My fact-finding drive is the key to my entire research career as well as the teaching to which I have dedicated so much of my life.

I drove to the hospital. After an hour, I had got permission to search the basement archives, and instructions from the nurse about how to find old sets of handwritten notes. When we found it, we placed the folder on a small table in the archive. A beam of light reached us through the narrow window above our heads. Yes, there it was. Ten years ago, I had had the same pattern of elevated liver values as now. It followed that the current results were probably not due to metastases in the liver.

I had a chance to survive. I didn't want to become too emotional about it and I was still in a dark space. But what was really going on? A week later, I had a new diagnosis: not liver cancer but chronic hepatitis. It was a great leap forward.

Two weeks after that, the lymph node results came in. The nodes showed no infiltration by cancer cells. No metastases? The second round of radiotherapy sessions was called off. Once more, everything was turning upside down—would life begin again now?

We moved back to our home in Hudiksvall. I went for hospital checkups monthly and then every second month. Time passed and the cancer did not recur.

Going back to work was surprisingly taxing. Many of my colleagues were not even aware that I had been ill. I met one of them in the elevator who exclaimed: "Are you back already?! How was Africa?" It was tiresome to inform each one in turn or, in some cases, to decide not to.

Life rumbled on and my desire to go to Mozambique grew stronger. A year passed. Now other questions had to be answered. Had the radiotherapy led to a full recovery? Would my new diagnosis of chronic liver disease affect my ability to cope with traveling to Africa and working there?

In the evenings, Agneta and I talked with deep, loving concern for each other. To travel or not to travel? How do we want to lead our lives? We both wanted to go. It was, we felt, what we were meant to do, and we had devoted so much of ourselves to preparing: our traveling in Asia, our professional training, our engagement with the ARO. If I had only a few more years to live, would it not be best to spend that time doing what we wanted?

Or perhaps we ought to stay at home and spend time with the children? People close to us tried to stop us from leaving Sweden.

In the end, we made the decision entirely independently of others. We would go.

Getting health insurance for me was a crucial factor. The oncologists decided that they could not underwrite the assurance of health that was required. I was referred to Folke Nordbring, head of the infectious diseases unit, where I had previously worked. I outlined the situation in a letter to Nordbring and he arranged for me to see him. When I entered his office, I was very conscious that this man's judgment would determine the rest of my professional life. However, I truly trusted Folke Nordbring and felt good simply to have my chances evaluated by a medic of his authority.

"Please take a seat. There's no need for a physical examination. We'll just have a talk. I have been through your notes already," he said and placed his right hand on the pile of documents on his desk.

He asked about the kind of work I would do in Mozambique and what the conditions would be like. Was it likely that I would be exposed to infectious diseases in contaminated food or water, or carried by mosquitoes or other insects? I answered yes to all these questions. If I fell ill, would I have access to effective healthcare? Doctors ready to treat me? Good laboratories? I answered no to all of these.

He nodded calmly and let me talk on. As I heard myself speaking, my mind told me I was on a hopeless quest.

Next, he asked why I wanted to work in such conditions. I explained that the recently independent Mozambique desperately needed qualified doctors and that I had spent a lot of time and effort preparing myself. Also, my wife was prepared to go and work as a midwife.

He kept looking at me but did not speak immediately. Then he said: "I can't see any reason why you shouldn't go. I will sign all the necessary forms."

Many years later, I met Folke again at an antibiotics conference in Vietnam. I sought him out to thank him for making that crucial decision. His first reaction surprised me: "Wow!" he exclaimed. "You're still alive!"

"Of course! I wanted to thank you for confirming that the radiotherapy had done the trick and I was well," I said. "It meant that I could go off to practice in Mozambique. And then carry on doing the international work I'm doing now."

"Look, Hans, I actually felt very dubious about signing a statement to say that you were well. I rather thought you might die pretty soon from an aggressive cancer. Or something. But I could see in your eyes that you truly wanted to go and work in the way you and your wife had been preparing yourselves for. So, I thought 'If he has only got a few more years, why shouldn't he go and do what he wants most of all?' That's why I wrote a fake assurance that enabled you to go to Mozambique."

Folke Nordbring had dared to take responsibility.

On October 23, 1979, Agneta, Anna, Ola, and I boarded the flight to Maputo, the capital of Mozambique.

3

To Nacala

It was afternoon when our plane landed in Maputo's modest airport. I looked around as we stepped into the hot air and saw palm trees. Strong sunlight was reflected off the pale cement of the runway. The children were so excited. On the journey we had been reading them crazy stories about Soda Pop written by the Swedish author Barbro Lindgren, until they had fallen asleep. Now they were ready for anything. My mother had made them each their own little rucksack and when we entered arrivals, they wanted to hold on to their own passports.

A Portuguese slogan had been painted on the side of the plane: "We carry not only passengers but solidarity." Indeed, about half the passengers were from aid organizations. People were flooding into Mozambique and we pompously called ourselves "solidarity workers."

Twelve years ago, I had promised the first leader of the Mozambican independence movement that I would go to his country and work as a doctor. A year earlier, I had been ready to keep my promise but been stopped by testicular cancer. If the children had not been so infectiously delighted with everything, sentiment might have overwhelmed me. Now, they left me no time to ponder.

The border officer checked our passports, looked over the two-year contracts issued by the Ministry of Health and welcomed us with a warm smile. Agneta and I knew that we would be working in medicine and midwifery but our contracts had given us no idea of where. We had agreed to be placed wherever the ministry thought we would be most needed. So, while we waited to pick up our luggage, the big question was: where to next?

We were met at the airport by Ninni Uhrus, our Swedish organization's local coordinator. Ninni had a perfect plan: she drove us straight to Maputo's only operational ice-cream parlor. The children's first African experience was eating ice cream in the shade of a parasol. It went down very well. It also gave me and Agneta time to ask questions.

We would be staying for a few days with a Norwegian couple, who had a child of Anna's and Ola's age and, importantly, a garden. Agneta and I should present ourselves at the Ministry of Health the following day to discuss our placement. The principle was never to send foreigners out without having interviewed them and asking every individual what they wanted.

"The officials don't behave like bureaucrats," Ninni told us.

The next day we were received by a charming woman from human resources who shared an office with several other civil servants. The health ministry was housed in a modernist building and the brown doors carried proper nameplates.

She had obviously studied our papers with care. Her first question concerned my cancer treatment. Was I well enough to work? Next: were our children happy about living in Mozambique? She came back to that question several times. We told her of our wish to go to Beira, where we had Swedish friends, and she took notes. Beira was the second largest city in the country and had a wonderful beach, which was particularly important to us. We knew that our work would be demanding, although we had no idea of just how hard it would be. To find a place that would be right for everyone in the family seemed critically important.

A few days later, we were back in the ministry, this time to meet a still more senior HR official. He was very direct—regrettably, at present there was no requirement for us anywhere near Beira. He would like us to move as soon as possible to the northern province of Nampula, more precisely to Nacala, the fourth-largest conurbation in the country and the busiest port. There was a desperate need there for doctors and midwives, both in the urban area and in the surrounding rural district. Later, I realized the ministry had planned all along to send us to Nacala but they recognized the need to meet us face-to-face first in order to judge whether we would be likely to cope with the pressure. I was still regarded as an inexperienced medic.

I would be working with Ana Edite, one of the country's few newly qualified doctors, who already worked in Nacala Porto. Having a colleague meant that I would only be on call alternate evenings, which would be a great advantage. We asked about living quarters but were told that the authorities in Nacala were dealing with that. Our last question: is there a beach? The official laughed, leaned forward and said: "You won't be disappointed. It's even better than in Beira."

He was right. For the next two years, the beach would be a joyous place of refuge for us.

Before leaving the building, we were handed our *guia de marcha* (marching orders): a document we had to present to the Nacala local authority. As in so many other aspects of life in Mozambique, the military terminology reflected both the past colonial order and the tensions between the newly independent state and some of its neighbors—notably, the South African apartheid regime and Rhodesia, where Ian Smith, leader of the white minority party, was still the prime minister. Both countries were racked by armed conflicts.

Our documents showed that we would be replacing a young Italian doctor who had asked to be moved after just one week in Nacala. It sounded worrying but we were reassured that he had arrived with a "naive and romantic" image of Africa, and had complained that "he had expected to live in the real Africa." The authorities in Nacala would have been understandably offended by the implication that large towns were not part of "real Africa."

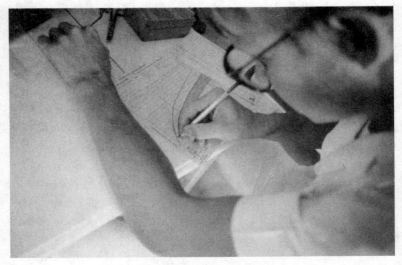

Filling in a growth chart

I met that young doctor a year later and he admitted that, at first, he had been rather naïve. However, the real reason he had asked to be moved was the exceptionally heavy workload. Nacala was a big town of about 85,000 people, while its large rural district had a population of more than 300,000. The entire area was served by one hospital with around fifty beds.

Within a few months, I would be the only doctor responsible for this gigantic community.

All that was in the future as we drove toward Nacala. Our first encounter with it was in the shape of a shantytown crowded with mud huts with straw roofs. It grew more densely populated the closer we got to the city center. The road was lined with cashew trees and palms, and, between the trees, paths wound their way in among the shanties.

We were on the high plateau but soon began to sense we were coming to the sea. On our right appeared the so-called Cement City, a wealthier part of Nacala, where villas and three- and four-story buildings had been built with cement produced by the town's own factory. Farther downhill the ocean spread itself out in front of us. The football field and the hospital were on one side of the bay, and high, forested hills rose on the other.

Nacala had a pharmacy and a post office but its health service was nowhere near adequate. As recently as fifteen years ago, the town had not really existed, so there were hardly any old houses and no one in the adult population had been born there.

We had been allocated a pleasant, one-story cement house. It needed some work, including an internal coat of paint, but because of the central planning system we were not allowed to pick our own color. There was just one option—pale blue.

Our part of town had been built for the Portuguese population in the years before independence. Along the road from our house to the hospital were rows of little shops selling mostly tools, a paint shop with hardly any goods for sale, and a coconut stall.

My doctor colleague, Ana, had told me firmly that I was to be driven to work. A car would come to collect me at ten to eight every morning. But the driver turned up almost an hour late on the first morning, so I decided I would walk to work from then on. The hospital staff protested but I insisted and I was thrilled as I set out the next morning: here I was, walking to my new job, and there was so much to see along the road.

Someone greeted me pleasantly before I reached the garden gate. Turning the first corner, I noticed that most of the other pedestrians, regardless of age, stopped when they saw me. There were a lot of people out and about, and everyone stared at me intently. When I was about to pass anyone, they greeted me politely. This carried on all the way to the hospital and, when I walked home in the evening, it happened all over again. The attention made me feel uncomfortable but I assumed people would get used to me. After a few days of staring and greeting, I asked Mama Rosa what was wrong with me. Mama Rosa, a midwife, had already become my closest friend among the staff. She was older than the rest, self-assured and experienced.

She laughed: "You are white. You shouldn't be walking. Ana told you to wait for the car."

I thought she must be exaggerating and convinced myself that people would get used to seeing me walking to work within another week.

Then I had a new idea. It came to me when I opened the enormous wooden crate full of our Swedish things—all possessions we had been recommended to pack before we left. It had been dispatched to Maputo by cargo ship in good time, Ninni had arranged for it to be transported to Nacala, and it arrived for our first weekend. It felt like Christmas for the whole family.

We spent the first Sunday in our new home unpacking our treasures. The children were overjoyed at finding their Lego. Agneta sorted out our clothes and I started to fit together the two bicycles I had taken apart as best I could. We had realized that our salaries

The large wooden crate has arrived

wouldn't stretch to buying a car and reckoned we might anyway be more easily accepted by our neighbors if we didn't come across as wealthier than everybody else. Some Mozambicans could afford cars but they were few and far between. Besides, we had bikes in Sweden and used them much more than our car. Reconstructing the bikes gave me a strong feeling of being at home and they worked just fine when I tested then in the garden. It was a happy family that went to bed after the first weekend in the new home.

Monday morning, I was late for work when I set out. Still, I had my bicycle and would cover the distance faster. As I swung out through the gate at speed, everything seemed to have fallen into place: my family had a house to live in and I was cycling to work.

It took me only a few seconds to grasp that the strangely powerful noise I heard from behind me was not a truck with a broken silencer—it was peals of laughter. I had to have a look. People in the street, who had greeted me so politely during the past week, were pointing at me and killing themselves laughing. As I cycled toward the hospital, those behind me called out to alert others. I saw grown women literally falling about laughing and twitching.

The laughter pursued me onto the main street. By then, I was deeply embarrassed. What was so amusing? I checked my flies, and that I had nothing in my hair or on my face that could attract attention. Probably blushing, I reacted by pedaling faster, but that was apparently even funnier. I passed a queue of patients and their relatives, waiting in the yard in front of the hospital. To a man and woman, they all collapsed, screaming with laughter. The noise was so loud that some of the hospital staff came running out before I got off the bike.

Luckily, as it turned out, Mama Rosa was among them. She didn't laugh and instead eyed me seriously. We retreated to the emergency reception area where we could talk in private for a moment. I was confused and at a loss, somewhere between laughter and tears.

"Why is everyone laughing at me?" I almost shouted.

"Why did you cycle to the hospital?" Mama Rosa replied.

"Because that's how I get to work in Sweden."

"You're working in Nacala now and here people have never seen an adult white man who cycles to work. No one from the hospital staff does. The Portuguese used to give bikes to their children. And, yes, there was one Portuguese man who lived uptown and used to cycle when he had had too much to drink."

"Come on, it makes sense for me to cycle. I'm not Portuguese. Besides, Mozambique is supposed to be independent now." I was close to becoming angry.

Mama Rosa put her hand on my arm and answered: "You must listen to me. It isn't about being sensible or not. You'll become a joke and then you won't function as a doctor here. I'll tell the cleaner, Ahmed, to wheel your bike back to your house. You can use it to take your children on outings but never again to get to the hospital. We must stop chatting now. I have a woman in the delivery room. She gave birth at home, the baby died and now she is very ill. She has tetanus."

Tetanus is a terrible affliction. I knew that I had to convince all the pregnant women here to be vaccinated and I would fail if I became known as the local clown. I had to choose. I decided that cycling was out of the question if it affected my credibility, especially when introducing new ways of protecting the population.

It would not be the last time I had to ask myself: which changes are most important? And which changes are easy to make?

A year later, we had succeeded with our vaccination program and no more women or newborn babies were arriving with tetanus symptoms. But I still couldn't cycle to work. A mantra had stuck in my mind: "At first, change only what must be changed. Let everything else wait."

* * *

My first friend from Africa, whom I'd met years before I moved there, would help me toward new ways of working and thinking. He came from a village in the countryside. His three older siblings had died as newborn infants. When he was born, his mother gave him the name Niheriwa. It was a temporary name—a kind of standby in the local culture, when it was feared that a child would soon die. It meant something like "the grave is waiting for you."

But Niheriwa had survived. His parents, who ran a small farm, worked hard and managed to keep the boy at school. He did exceptionally well. Throughout his life, Niheriwa kept his "temporary" name because, he told me, he wanted to honor his hardworking mother and remember that all life is fragile.

Niheriwa became fluent in ten languages and was so successful at school that he was accepted at a Catholic seminary, expecting to be ordained. He ran away from the seminary as soon as the struggle for an independent Mozambique began, and walked all the way to Dar es Salaam in Tanzania, to enroll at the independence movement FREMILO's headquarters to join the fight for freedom.

We were in contact for the first time in 1967, when he replied to a letter I had sent to FRELIMO, asking for information. After he had been working in the office for a few years, Niheriwa's ability was noticed and he was offered the opportunity to study in East Germany. We had kept up a sporadic correspondence and he had visited me in Sweden during his student years in Europe. He eventually graduated as a qualified mining engineer, one of the very first from Mozambique in Germany.

Chance brought us together again in 1979. My family and I were queuing in Maputo air terminal to check in for the flight to Nacala and just moving on when I spotted Niheriwa in the next queue along. We hugged and greeted each other happily.

"But where are you going to live?" Niheriwa asked.

"In Nacala."

"Then I'll come and see you!"

Niheriwa had just returned home and was going to take up a post as director of a mine in his native province. As a big port city, Nacala was where imports for and exports from the mine would be shipped.

He came to see us regularly over the subsequent years. Niheriwa was a tall, heavily built man. His expressive face constantly changed, shifting through a whole range of feeling, from great seriousness to vivacious humor. He was a good, dependable friend and advised me on many things. He taught me a trick to stop ambulance drivers from cheating the hospital by trading unused spare parts for old ones. Above all, Niheriwa guided me in the extremely tough task of being the boss of a crew of people in a very poor country, where hardly anyone had the training required for the job they were employed to do.

He also explained why I shouldn't keep talking all the time. The best thing, he said, is to stay silent and let other people talk. Ask questions but focus on listening to what people say in reply and try to get to what really troubles them. Once everyone has had a chance to speak, the boss should think things over. The pause will make his staff nervous but, when he breaks the silence, he will tell them he understands what they have said and that this is what they, as a team, will do. Then he will describe how it will be done. Niheriwa insisted this was how to become accepted as the leader and establish discipline.

One weekend, when Niheriwa was staying with us, we went to the beach. Nacala has one of the best deep-water harbors on the east coast of Africa. A curving peninsula creates a wide, protected bay where even the largest ships can enter the harbor. One of the Indian Ocean's most wonderful beaches is a little farther along and it was our goal that day.

When we arrived, we parked in the shade of a pine tree, climbed out of the car and took in the view of the many hundreds of meters of sunlit beach in front of us. There were more people on the beach than usual, maybe twenty families.

"It's a shame that this place is so busy today," I said to Niheriwa, who was standing next to me. "Let's quickly try to find somewhere peaceful."

He sighed heavily, grabbed my arm and got serious: "Look over there at Nacala, with its more than 80,000 inhabitants, just a few kilometers from where we are. Roughly half the population of the city are children but here, maybe forty children are on the beach. One child in every thousand! You call that too many? When I was a student in Germany, I'd often go to the Baltic coast near Rostock. Every weekend, the beaches would be full of children, many thousands of them, playing with their friends and family, and having a great time."

Then he let go of my arm, walked to the car and helped our children carry their toys and swim fins. I picked up the rug and the sun umbrella and Agneta took the picnic basket. We only had to walk a short distance to find a place to settle on what was actually an almost empty beach.

Time and time again, my African colleagues have surprised me by demonstrating how my mind keeps following the same thought patterns as most Europeans when they arrive in Africa. Their intentions and Niheriwa's were the same: to remind me (and all of us Europeans) that, however engaged we are in the struggle to free Africa of misery, we seem hopelessly lost when faced with an Africa where people have the same dreams for their lives as we do for ours. Why should it be so hard to accept that most families, wherever they live in the world, want good lives for themselves? Want to holiday in faraway places? Spend contented, relaxing days on the beach?

One day in the hospital, late in the afternoon, an elderly woman with a leg fracture arrived, carried in by her two sons. She had not managed to get out of the way in time when a tree was felled in her village. The ends of the broken bone were protruding through her skin and I would have to force them back into place. The infection risk was serious, and potentially fatal. It would be difficult to get the bones joined up properly, especially since we had no X-ray machine and had just run out of anesthetics. She was warned that the treatment would be very painful. I cleaned the wound carefully. Two staff nurses then took hold of the patient under her armpits to pull her in one direction, while the strongest junior nurse was told to pull the foot in the opposite direction. After much grappling I managed to line up the fracture surfaces so that they fitted and supported each other. I closed the wound, stitched the skin margins and put the entire limb in a plaster cast, from groin to toes. Finally, because the wound would have to be dressed, I removed the area of plaster covering it. The procedure had taken two hours and had caused the patient intense pain. I left instructions that she was to be put on an antibiotics drip, and told her that she had to stay in bed for a week and not put any weight on the leg.

That evening, I went home feeling a certain sense of accomplishment. The treatment had been an orthopedic procedure far beyond my technical qualifications.

When I arrived at the hospital the following morning the first person I saw was the old woman. She was standing in the doorway, waving to me. Upset, I rushed to speak to her.

"You must stay in bed," I said in Portuguese.

But she only understood the local language Makua, so I tried to explain in sign language. A tearful nurse had been trying to persuade the patient to get back to bed. She translated what the patient was saying: her hens might get stolen so she had to get back home.

"Look, the cast is strong," the old lady said, banging her foot on the floor for emphasis.

*The entire hospital staff in front of the clinic—qualified
medical staff in white and untrained staff in blue.*

* * *

When I looked down at her foot, I discovered that something had gone very wrong: the immobilized foot was pointing sideways instead of forward, as it should. At the back of my mind, I heard the consultant surgeon's warning from when I trained in orthopedics: "Check alignment before you put on a plaster cast. With a broken leg, get the relationship right between foot and knee. A patient in pain tends to twist the upper part of the leg inward. You have to pull the bits into their proper place before putting on the plaster."

I had made a classic mistake and fixed the foot pointing outward. I felt terrible that I had done this.

Curious patients and their relatives stood in a ring around us, watching and giggling once they realized that the old lady's foot was pointing the wrong way. I asked the nurse to translate my advice: I would have to remove the plaster, pull the leg into the correct position and put on a new cast. I twisted my right foot outward and lumbered about, surrounded by sniggering onlookers, as an animated illustration of how she would be limping for the rest of her life if she didn't let me reset her foot.

But when I was done with my performance, the old lady smilingly put her hand on my arm. The nurse translated again.

"Doctor, what you're showing is as much as I ever hoped to be able to do. I can feed my chickens and take care of my grandchildren. I am happy to have survived. To walk about like that is fine. Not to worry, you have other patients to cure today. I just came along to get some pills from the nurse and then wait for you so I could thank you before I go home."

The people around us nodded and mumbled in agreement as she shook my hand. Then they stepped aside to let her cross the sandy yard in front of the hospital entrance. Almost fifty of us looked on as her footsteps in the sand formed a trail like the track of a large tractor tire.

I never saw her in the hospital again but learned later she had survived. The plaster had cracked and fallen off after a month and her foot was badly out of line. Still, her chickens were all right, so she could give her grandchildren eggs to eat now and then.

Patients, relatives, and the hospital staff taught me how to put up with the knowledge that I could not achieve everything I set out to do. Also—one of hardest things for me to accept—that, in the end, it was up to the patient. Slowly, I grasped that everyone, even the poorest, who were often the most superstitious, was fundamentally wise when faced with the toughest decisions of their lives.

My mentor, Ingegerd Rooth, who had been a mission doctor all her life, had told me: "When you work in a place of extreme poverty, don't try to do things perfectly. All you will accomplish is wasting time and resources that could be put to better use." In effect, this was the same lesson that the old lady with her broken leg had taught me.

That lesson generated a new way of working: the two-by-two table. The idea crystalized for me about a month later, on a Sunday night after another marvelous day on the beach. I had read the children a bedtime story and gone into the sitting room to work. It was a reasonably cool evening and there was no need for the fan to be on. I settled down at the cleared dinner table and started to look over the past week's "de-stressing list."

I had taken to carrying a small notebook in my pocket and grabbing whatever pen was at hand to write down a word or a brief phrase as a method for staying calm whenever I identified something that I felt must be changed in the provision of care or the structure of the organization. At first, my insistence on instantly correcting anything I thought out of order had made me unbearable to the people I was working with, and to myself as well. The solution I had arrived at was to confine myself to writing everything down.

That Sunday night, I planned to go through my notes and prioritize the things that needed to be changed. I began by writing a clean copy of the list of problems I had come across. Some problems were insoluble and I crossed these out at once. Next, I needed to resolve the rest of the problems. I drew a large square divided into four fields on a sheet of paper and wrote EASY and HARD over the two vertical columns. To the left of the two horizontal rows, I wrote IMPORTANT and NOT IMPORTANT. Now I could fit my notes into four groups. After pondering for some twenty minutes, the upper left field, EASY and IMPORTANT, contained four items. The first one was "separate the dressing of clean and infected wounds in outpatients' minor injuries clinic."

On Monday, I planned to have a word with Papa Enrique, the hospital's oldest nursing assistant and a very kind man.

That Monday, I crossed the hospital yard after the morning ward round and entered Papa Enrique's small premises, located in the middle of the long building that housed outpatient care. His was probably the only space in the entire hospital that did not smell bad. Everywhere else, the air was stale or worse. Some patients had suppurating wounds or rotting body parts. Others simply had no facilities for washing their clothes. Some of the bedridden patients did not get a bedpan in time. Relatives who came to help with feeding spilled food on the floor. Everyone, whether wearing shoes or not, brought in sand because the whole town was sandy underfoot. The need for cleaning was constant but our resources only sufficient for one daily round by the cleaners. We lacked effective ventilation and while some days could be suffocatingly hot, air humidity was too high for the towels to dry on the washing line during the rainy season. Despite all this, we fought to keep up appearances and had agreed there should be vases with freshly picked flowers in all the windows.

Going into Papa Enrique's treatment room, the strong smell of cleaning fluid hit my nostrils the moment the door opened. On one side of the room, around a dozen patients were lined up on a low wooden bench, waiting to be seen. On the other side, a patient sat on a tall table covered by a stained, once-white plastic sheet. Papa Enrique leaned over him, bandaging his hand.

He straightened up at once and greeted me pleasantly. I told him that I had a small change in mind: to organize his patients so that he could attend to the clean wounds first and then move on to the infected ones. He looked troubled and said he wasn't sure what I meant by clean wounds being different to infected ones. My attempts to explain got us nowhere, so I told him to finish the bandaging and then I'd show him the difference.

Two of the waiting patients had lower leg wounds, and I asked them to sit next to each other on the bench. One of them had a recent, substantial burn. His face looked pained as he told me how he had knocked over a large pan of boiling water that morning.

"This wound isn't infected and it is very important you don't cause an infection when you clean and bandage it," I instructed Papa Enrique.

Then I turned to the second man with a lower leg wound. At the upper edge of the wound, pus flowed from a small hole. His was a tragic case of osteomyelitis. The pus was forming inside the infected bone and draining steadily through a fistula, a channel through the tissues.

I asked Papa Enrique if he could see the difference between the large but superficial blisters on the burned skin and the small hole where the pus was coming out.

He inspected the wounds carefully, looked up at me and said in a worried tone: "I can't see any hole."

"What are you talking about?" I almost shouted. "Can't you see the hole with the pus coming out?"

"No, doctor. I don't see so well anymore," he answered quietly.

I was quite taken aback. Then I remembered that my glasses had quite strong lenses because I had been farsighted since childhood. I put my glasses on Papa Enrique. He glanced at the legs of the two patients and gestured with both arms—now it was his turn to speak almost at shouting pitch:

"Now I see it! That one has just blisters but here there's pus coming from a small hole."

He took the glasses off, looked again and then held them up to me, exclaiming: "Without these, I can't see the hole."

I brought my spare glasses back after lunch and gave them to Papa Enrique, who thanked me very warmly. The gift was hugely important to him. I interrupted his flow of polite gratitude to show him something.

"Take a look at these two sets of notes. This is what I'm going to write for every patient before I send him or her along to you for wound dressing."

The messages were straightforward: one said CLEAN WOUND, and the other said DIRTY WOUND. I handed both notes to Papa Enrique, who took them but looked troubled again.

"It's really not at all difficult; don't worry," I said. The room was empty for a moment and I pointed at the bench, explaining that everyone with a clean wound would be seen first. Every morning, patients with dirty wounds had to wait until those with clean ones had been looked after. Between every batch, the bench should be cleaned with strong disinfectant.

By now, deep furrows had formed on Papa Enrique's forehead. Embarrassed, he murmured his answer: "Doctor, I've something else to tell you. I can't read."

I had been working in the hospital for nearly three months but had failed to realize that almost all the assistants were illiterate. I had just taken a step on the long road toward understanding the complexities of social underdevelopment.

Later that afternoon I complained to Mama Rosa but she cut me short.

"I thought you understood what it was like in the colonial era. Most Mozambicans had no chance of going to school. Those who learned to read landed better jobs than assistant nurse. These days, many attend literacy classes in the evenings. Give us a few more years. Then all the staff will be able to read, even Papa Enrique, especially now that you have given him a pair of glasses. Because if you can't afford glasses, you can't learn to read either," she added.

In the same month that Papa Enrique got his glasses, one of my days at work ended with me filling up our dark green Land Rover with patients. It was at this time the only vehicle we had to help us look after more than 300,000 people (at other times we had two) and tonight we were using it to take several acutely ill patients to the regional hospital in Nampula. It was a two-hundred-kilometer drive and the road, though partly paved, was studded with potholes. To make this particular journey worse, it was raining heavily.

Regardless, the car had to leave as soon as possible because it would be carrying patients afflicted by illnesses I could not deal with in Nacala. One of them was a man suffering from schizophrenia. He had arrived the day before in a florid, psychotic, hallucinating state. His family had grown very scared, tied him up and brought him to the hospital. He needed to be cared for in the psychiatric unit in Nampula. All I could do was give him massive doses of sedative until he was passive and drowsy. Later, he almost lost consciousness, but I had to keep him sedated while we waited for other very ill patients to join us. It took time but I could not send the car off with one patient at a time. The psychotic man would have to stay overnight.

A woman arrived the following day, pregnant and nearly fullterm. She was bleeding and I suspected that a low-placed placenta was blocking the passage for the baby's head. Unless the baby was taken out by caesarean section, she would bleed to death once her contractions started. I made her wait, too, because the Land Rover could hold three patients, and another acutely ill patient might well turn up in the next few hours.

Later that afternoon, a middle-aged man came in with a bad complication to a hernia. The patient had been ignoring the bulge in his left groin for ten years. Now, his intestines had begun to twist themselves around each other, a condition that would likely kill him within twelve to twenty-four hours. He urgently needed an operation. Time for the Land Rover to go.

The driver had it all worked out. The drowsy man would sit in the front passenger seat. The man with the hernia would be on a stretcher in the back, across the seat. The pregnant woman and her relative would sit on the two remaining seats at the back. The relative promised to help the hernia patient when he threw up.

Why would we agree to take the pregnant woman's relative, an elderly woman, rather than a nurse? The simple reason was that the patient refused to go to a large hospital in a town she had never visited unless the other woman came with her. Mama Rosa decided that the relative should be allowed to go along.

Once the patients' few belongings had been packed, the vehicle was full. I checked that the driver had a full tank and that the nurse had given the psychotic patient a top-up dose of sedative. As the sun set, our only health-service vehicle was rolling down the main street to begin its three-hour journey to Nampula. Once I had checked that there were no other acute cases to deal with in the hospital, I went home for a calming family supper, hoping the bigger hospital would save my patients. I needed a good night's sleep. It was still raining and I fell asleep to the sound of drumming raindrops.

Knock knock knock, I heard in my dream. Then I realized that someone was actually hammering on our front door. I pulled on a dressing gown, switched the light on, undid the safety chain and peered outside. A man was standing in the rain. His eyes lit up when he saw me.

"Good evening, doctor," he said.

I took in the surprising fact that Manuel, our driver, had returned. "Are you back from Nampula already?" I said.

"No, *senhor*, I'm bringing this tire back. It had a puncture. I need you to help me fix the puncture tonight because I don't think those people can wait until the morning," he said, indicating the car tire held under his arm.

Utterly baffled, I asked where the car was. He had left it on the far side of the dam, he said, only fifteen kilometers outside Nacala but still in the middle of the countryside.

"Where are the patients?" I almost screamed.

"Oh, they're all there, inside."

"Inside what?"

"The car. The old *mama* said I had to hurry because her daughter had started bleeding again. That's why I thought it better to wake you up, doctor."

Manuel explained that it had taken a long time to get the tire off because he didn't have a screwdriver.

"Why not put on the spare tire?" I asked.

"This *is* the spare. I drove on it. Don't you remember me saying last month we needed a new inner tire? It hasn't arrived yet."

By now, the situation was clear in all its horror. My three critically ill patients were stranded inside a car in the middle of nowhere during a stormy night.

I dressed, packed a screwdriver and the damaged tire into our private car and drove to the port, which was open round the clock. I chased up the harbormaster and, after taking the time to brief me on his family's health issues, he agreed to get a mechanic from the port's machine workshop to repair the tire. He left me to supervise the work while he went off to find help with transport. He got hold of a truck just about to leave for Nampula despite the pouring rain. An hour later, Manuel and the repaired tire had joined the truck driver in his cabin. I drove home to snatch some sleep.

The next afternoon Manuel returned. I was very relieved to learn that all my patients had arrived at the regional hospital alive.

It was consistently difficult to foresee the different ways that having very limited resources would impact us. Insufficient transport for fuel and medicine, and a lack of skilled staff and decent equipment, didn't just hamper our ability to achieve what we set out to do; it made it almost impossible to even predict what might be achievable.

On the evening of the day I almost died, I squeezed into the Suzuki jeep, perched on a board between the driver and the front passenger. We had been to a very useful Friday meeting with the regional health service bosses and the heads of each of the eighteen districts in Nampula. A few other medics and I had nagged the organizers to be allowed to go home that night. My only other medically trained colleague in Nacala, Ana Edite, was also with us. We had bought sacks of flour and avocados in the market and packed them away in the car.

The road, which came from Malawi, crossed northern Mozambique and ran all the way to Nacala. It was in relatively good condition but rainwater that had gathered in the massive potholes was spilling over and washing the road's shoulders away. All along the road, there were scattered villages surrounded by cassava fields without boundary ditches. It was like driving through a forest of low willow shrub.

Cassava, a fast-growing bush, has edible roots, which are a basic foodstuff in many tropical countries, including Mozambique. The roots have a high starch content but can be toxic unless a lengthy preparation process is carried out properly.

The horizon was ringed by beautiful hills shaped like sugar cones and just a few hundred meters high. I felt these hills had been there since the beginning of time.

The driver was an electrician without a driver's license who was half asleep at the wheel and drove at 110 kilometers an hour. About halfway to Nacala, we were held up because a bridge had collapsed. About fifty meters before the gorge, traffic had been redirected by means of the usual local device—a large pile of twigs and branches. It had to do the job of more conventional road signs because tin signage was always instantly stolen.

In this case, to emphasize the danger ahead, the workmen had added a half-meter-high mud wall running across the road. In this part of Mozambique, the soil is a deep reddish-brown. I was always amazed to see how lovely bare, wet earth looked at sunset.

We had been zooming along in the darkness. Our driver missed the first warning and when I caught sight of the roadblock, we were just thirty meters away from it. I simply howled, unable to find the words in Portuguese.

All our driver had time to do was to twist the wheel. Then he lost control, so that when the car crashed into the mud embankment it was already in a skid. The car rotated and leaped into the air at the same time with a momentum so powerful I was subjected to a centrifugal force. I did not feel upside down, even as the world turned. Green grass up there, dark starry sky down there.

We flew through the air. I'll die now. I had time to think these words.

Seconds later I was amazed not to have been crushed. The impact had not come. Instead, the car kept gliding on its roof like a surfboard on water. The wet grass and soft mud did nothing to stop it. The forward movement made me shoot out through the gap where the windscreen had been and then continue sliding on my back. Nothing made sense. A few moments later and I was lying quietly in the tall grass. I slowly pushed myself upright with my hands and found myself staring straight into the beams of the headlights. The car's engine was still running.

My mind fixated on my right foot. It was bare, and the nail of the big toe had gone. My left foot was still clad in its sock and shoe. Almost without thinking, I began to walk toward the car. I came across my right shoe. I put it on. Then I spotted my glasses and put them on. Then, for the first time, I thought about the car. The light glowed, the engine was turning and it was upside down. It will catch fire and then explode, I thought. I had seen what happens in films. Cars overturn and a little later they explode.

So far, I had not had time to reflect on being, seemingly, in one piece. I went to the driver's side, saw it was empty and stuck my hand in to turn the ignition off. Silence fell.

A calm voice spoke near me: "Why turn it off? It's completely dark now."

It was a doctor from one of the other districts. While I had been getting up from the grass and putting on my lost shoe, he had crawled out through the rear door and been able to talk to the others. They were also all right. We noted that the driver was gone. He had run away.

"Three of us have got away with only minor injuries," my colleague said. "They are sitting behind the car."

Now we heard wailing from inside the car. Ana Edite was stuck in there, under our sacks of flour and avocados, squashed up against the roof bars. Our shopping was scattered all over and around Ana and our first thought was to get her out by getting it out. We tried to push the car from side to side but Ana screamed in a way that made us realize that was a terrible idea. Then it struck me that we could dig her out of the soft mud. I dug with the help of a key I had found in a pocket. When she had unstuck a little, we slowly pulled her forward, feet first.

Then we stood there in the middle of the night. It could be half an hour between cars on this road in the Mozambican countryside.

The people who lived in the huts on the other side of the road came out with paraffin lamps so we could have a closer look at people's injuries. I examined Ana, who said she had bad abdominal pain on the left side. I understood that she was bleeding internally, as I sat with her, checking her pulse while we waited for a car. Her pulse rate was increasing, as it would initially if the patient was losing a lot of blood.

I looked for damage on her body, including on her fingers and face and under her hair. I couldn't find anything and could not do anything for her. This is a matter of luck, I thought. If she is unlucky, she will die quickly. If she is lucky, we will get her to a hospital in time.

"They are on the way, and they'll take you to Nampula," I told her, to calm her down.

"My husband, you must get in touch with him," Ana said.

Then a car did come along. One of my colleagues, who was only a few kilometers from his own hospital in Monapo, knew the family in the car. Later the same night, Ana Edite was on the operating table. She had years of rehabilitation to come, and a poorly functioning foot that she would have to cope with for the rest of her life. But she survived.

I had been so grateful to the villagers who had crossed the road to light us with their paraffin lamps that I tried to give them a sack of avocados as a thank-you gift. A crazy idea, Ana Edite's husband told me much later. Every one of them was a small-scale avocado grower, he explained, laughing heartily.

I cursed myself that night because by helping to arrange the transport I had broken a rule I knew only too well: you should never drive at night in a poor country and especially not after heavy rain. I had lost several friends that way. However, it was a relief to know that Agneta was not waiting anxiously for me at home. She did not expect me until lunchtime the following day. I slept at my colleague's house, and in the morning washed my foot and rinsed my torn shirt.

When I was dropped off outside our house, Agneta was standing in front of the open kitchen door, smiling. Tears welled up in my eyes as it struck me how close to death I had come. We stood, holding each other tightly, just inside the door. But that intense moment was not to last because there was a knock on the front door. Irritated, Agneta went to see who it was.

In trooped the Grupos Dinamizadores, the local group of Party reps. They turned up on people's doorsteps on Saturdays to check that everyone had tidied up properly. The point was to avoid being found out as a *xiconhoca*—that is, a filthy counter-revolutionary who was probably trading on the black market.

Agneta tried to explain that this was not a good time for an inspection but the Grupos Dinamizadores paid no attention to her. They told me to go and rest in bed instead of standing there trying to explain things to them, so I lay in bed sobbing while they poked about all over the house. In the end, they took an interest in only one thing: the sack of avocados. This was understandable, because it was an unusual find: we had never during our two years in Nacala been able to buy avocados in the town. Had we acquired it on the black market?

As this utterly absurd night and day drew to a close, I was struck by a fact that would become critical for our entire continued existence in Nacala. The thought crept into my mind when I had calmed down after a few hours at home: Ana Edite would not be coming back to work. I would be the only doctor in the whole district. I would be on call round the clock.

The health service's resources were already minimal and the care needs maximal. From that day on, as I went to work in the mornings, I thought more and more often about how different the health statistics were in Sweden. My thinking followed these lines: "Today, my day's work will be the equivalent of the work of a hundred doctors in Sweden. What am I to do? Examine each patient a hundred times faster or pick one out of every hundred patients?"

Every day, I somehow had to find a compromise between these two options.

As a matter of fact, very many sick people never saw the inside of any care facility, let alone the hospital. True, it was rather small with its fifty or so beds, which were always full. Some inpatients even had to lie on the floor. Still, what care we could offer was not limited by the number of beds. The real limitation was us, the staff—in quantity as well as quality. I had a little more than two years of professional experience. The handful of Mozambican nurses had four years at school and then trained in nursing for one year. More than half of the rest of the staff were illiterate.

If this had been Sweden, I would have been one of a hundred medics responsible for the care of this population. Also, the child mortality rate would have been a hundred times smaller. My challenge now was to get a grip on what our resources actually were and how to use them in the best possible way. Beyond the hospital, it was harder still to get my head around the nearly nonexistent care resources for the rural population. Practically all of them lived in conditions of extreme poverty. Their strength and energy were concentrated on finding enough to eat and, even then, there were many days when they would go without.

Again and again, I was forced to recognize how unrealistic my ambitions were. Everyone, patients as well as hospital staff, tried hard to show me what was possible and reasonable. It was very far below the level of expectation that my Swedish medical education had instilled in me. A need one hundred times greater than in Sweden had to be met using one percent of the resources. That meant about ten thousand times less resource per patient. Ten thousand!

I admit that trying to adjust to and cope with this differential felt like being in a post-traumatic state. I called it "my four-zeros brain trauma."

The psychological state of generalized scarcity taught me lessons about myself. I had previously thought that I led my life guided by certain unshakable values. I believed, for instance, that you must not kill a thief. That is, until I was pushed beyond control. One night, someone unscrewed the headlight covers on one of our two ambulances and stole the bulbs. Now that ambulance could not be used after dark. That theft filled me with an explosive hatred. I fear that I might have killed the thief if I had caught him. Just as I might have killed the creep who stole our ducks.

The children enjoyed the ducks but our main reason for keep-

In a school room, with the children

ing them was to have a small but valuable source of meat in a centrally managed economy with erratic supplies of food. One night, the ducks were screeching so loudly that the row woke Agneta. She looked out through a window and saw someone breaking into the duck house. She called out and the thief ran away. I jumped into the car and chased him. When I spotted him in front of me on the road, I put my foot down and followed him around a corner. An echo was bouncing around in my head: "That bastard won't get our ducks." Until I realized that I was about to run him down and kill him. I must pull myself together. The thief slipped into a side path and disappeared. He was lucky. The judicial system was failing and people often took justice into their own hands, sometimes brutally. Theft caused immeasurable damage to people and the punishments could be vile. One common method was to tie the thief's hands behind his or her back with lengths of rubber cut from inner car tires. Unless someone cut the straps quickly, the blood stopped circulating and the hands became permanently useless. I had quite a few people with tied-up hands coming into the hospital and was normally furious at having to waste time on them.

The cruel dangers of living in extreme poverty were also reflected in other injuries we had to deal with in the hospital. The town had only one shop which sold food, the *loja do povo* or "people's shop," and its shelves were often empty. Now and then, it got a consignment of fish, which was sold via the loading bay because the goods entrance had a big steel door. The pressure of the crowd of customers would have been enough to break the display windows if they had traded as usual. Instead, the shop manager opened the steel door and admitted some fifty people at a time. The crowd soon became chaotic, and someone always got badly squashed. On days when several bone fractures were queuing at the hospital to be fixed, we knew that the state shop had been selling fish or sugar.

*   *   *

The car stopped outside our house and our Swedish friends were still laughing as they climbed out. It had been easy to find us.

"We did just what you said and asked people where the doctor lived. They all pointed to the right place at once!"

They were a couple of about our age who had come to stay with us for the weekend. The same organization that had recruited us had recently arranged for them to come to Mozambique and work in the large regional hospital in Nampula, two hundred kilometers from Nacala. The husband had a post as the pediatric doctor on the neonatal unit.

It was fantastic to have visitors. We were hungry for conversation and especially keen to talk to people who could understand how we lived now. Lunch went on and on because we had so much to discuss. We spent a lot of time comparing our places of work.

"Honestly, none of my nurses have any specialist qualifications," he told me.

"Half of my staff can't read," I said. And so it went. We kept talking past each other in a rather male way.

We unquestionably worked with very different levels of staffing and equipment. That was how it had to be, because the regional hospital also taught clinical students, so the care had to be of a reasonable standard.

Our talk was interrupted by an energetic knock on our front door. Because the telephone was out of order, a nurse's assistant had walked from the hospital to fetch me. A very ill child had just been admitted.

My friend borrowed a white coat from me and came with me in the car. When we stepped into the small room for acute admissions, we met the terrified eyes of a mother trying to breastfeed an emaciated infant. The baby girl, who was only a few months old, was almost unconscious and her eyes were sunken. Bad diarrhea, the nurse told me. When I pressed the skin over the child's belly using two fingers, the fold persisted long after I had taken my fingers away. The diagnosis was obvious: she was dying from dehydration and was too weak to suckle. I took a thin tube, introduced it via her nose into her stomach and told the nurse which type of fluid replacement to use and how much.

My friend was shocked. When I was almost done, I felt his hand gripping my shoulder and he pulled me out of the small room, stopped outside in the corridor, and looked at me with an infuriated expression.

"What you just did was utterly unethical! That baby did not get the right treatment. You'd never have done it to your own child. She was very sick and should have been hooked up to an intravenous drip immediately. You are risking her life by giving rehydration solution via a nasogastric tube. She could start vomiting it up and lose the water and salts she needs to survive. I suppose you're taking the quick way out because you want to get to the beach before supper."

He was unprepared for the kind of medicine that the brute facts had forced me to accept.

"No, what you saw is the standard treatment in this hospital. This is how we work. We never do better, because of the resources and the staff we have. And that includes me. I have to get home in time for supper at least a few evenings every week, otherwise neither I nor my family would make it through another month. It might take me half an hour to get a drip set up for this child. And there's a high risk that the nurse won't be up to keeping an eye on it and the baby will get no fluid at all. But the nurse can do tube rehydration, it's more straightforward. You must accept that our level of care is only as good as possible."

"No, I can't," my friend insisted. "It is unethical to manage that baby with fluid fed by nasogastric tube. I am going to put her on an IV drip and you can't stop me."

I didn't stop him. Instead I brought him the thin needles suitable for the veins of small children. We had saved some up in a cupboard in the doctors' office. Despite many attempts, my friend could not get a needle into any of the baby's veins. Next, he wanted the necessary equipment for incising, to expose a deep blood vessel. He set about this minor operation and our nurse did her best to assist him. I left them to it, went home and had supper with my family and my friend's partner. My work recently had been relentless and I had not eaten an evening meal at home for several days.

Afterward, I drove back to the hospital to pick up my friend. After much effort, he had finally got the drip up and running. The baby seemed a little better but still would not suckle.

That evening brought no rest. Once the children were asleep, my friend and I sat on the sofa and talked deeply and very honestly about the ethics of what we were doing.

"You must always do your best for each and every patient who wants to be seen," he said.

Numbers are so important in ethical discussions. It is misleadingly easy to define what is right and wrong when you speak about one patient at a time.

"I don't think so," I replied. "It is unethical to spend all available resources, including time, on trying to save only those who have been admitted to the hospital."

I went on to explain that more childhood deaths would probably be avoided if I spent more time on improving health facilities at street level—that is, care in local health centers and small clinics. My task must be to do all I could to improve child survival and health in the entirety of the town and its surroundings. I had become convinced that most of those who died from preventable causes had stayed at home and never come to the hospital. If we were to concentrate all our resources on making the hospital as good as possible, fewer children would be vaccinated, fewer competent members of staff would serve in the existing health centers, and the effect would be that, overall, more children would die. I was as responsible for the children I did not see suffer and die as for those I did see. Given our poor resources, I therefore had to live with the low level of care we offered at the hospital.

My friend disagreed, as most hospital doctors—and probably the majority of the public—would. He insisted that a doctor must do everything in his or her power for every patient they encounter.

"The supposition that you might be able to save more children somewhere else is simply a cruel theoretical guess," he said.

At about this stage in our debate, I stopped arguing but thought: "It cannot be more ethical to act on your instincts than to make a thorough investigation into how and where you can save most lives."

This thought stayed with me throughout the following day, as I tried to help a woman give birth. Her labor was into its second day. The baby was stuck. Its arm had been jammed and someone had tugged at it in an attempt to get the baby out. Now, the arm had grown dark for lack of blood supply. The hand was ruined and would have to be amputated. I could pick up the fetal heart sounds, so the child was still alive, but the mother was running a high temperature. Her uterus might rupture at any time.

I examined her and realized the baby's head had engaged in the birth canal. I could feel it just a few centimeters up. I had to hurry.

As a delivery progresses, the clinician—usually the midwife—has to check various functions hourly and enter the data into a so-called partograph. I had made my own partograph with a rule in mind that said: the sun must never rise twice on a woman giving birth. My version was a sheet of paper painted black for nights and left white for days. On the ward round, you tore off a piece of the day or the night. When the sheet of paper was gone, you had to act.

Labor that was continuing when the third twenty-four-hour span was about to begin meant declaring war—the baby must get out somehow. The mother was correspondingly a war victim requiring emergency surgery, and I was a war medic practicing the medicine of the disaster zone. My job in Nacala forced me to work in that spirit from time to time.

"Now what do I do?" I thought.

It was clear to me that I was going to have to kill the baby to save the mother. More specifically, I was going to have to carry out an extraction by dismembering the fetus. I had no proper instruments so I went in with a closed pair of scissors and drove their tips into the fontanelle. The skull came apart and the fetal brain fell out. The baby was now dead. I applied clamps to open up the passage and managed to get the child out, arm first, without the mother's uterus rupturing. Next, it was crucial to fix a catheter in her bladder. Otherwise the mother ran the risk of developing a cloaca—a breach in the wall separating the vagina from the anal canal, which would allow feces to pass out through the vagina. One usually fixes the catheter by inflating a balloon once it is inside the bladder, but this time I had to be very careful. I used stitches to hold it in place.

The mother was looked after as carefully as possible. And she made it. When well enough, she returned home to her other children. However, having to kill a viable full-term fetus in order to extract it and save the mother is very demanding and very challenging. Did I make the right decision?

Yes, it was the right thing to do in this case. Learning how to make such judgments is hard but it is much harder to act accordingly. Labor is especially dramatic. When the process begins, you are with a healthy woman longing to see the child she loves. Forty-eight hours later she is in deepest hell and close to death.

What to do for her? And what not to do? To dare to make these decisions in the moment, it is crucial that you have explained to yourself exactly which principles you will act on: why your choices will be such as they are. I was appalled at what I had had to do to save this mother, but I knew it was the right decision.

At the same time, thinking back to the dehydrated baby of the previous night, I recognized that, for me, it had become a grim necessity to compare the number of deaths in two groups of children: Nacala children who had been brought to the hospital versus those who were kept at home. Despite our limitations, we had improved the care we offered those who were seen in our hospital, and the proportion of children dying was slowly declining. People seemed to have noticed this, because the number of children we saw was steadily increasing. Most of them suffered from life-threatening conditions such as malaria, pneumonia, and diarrhea. Often, they were weakened by malnutrition, which was far too common, as well as by anemia due to hookworm infections.

Over a year, about a thousand children stayed in the hospital, roughly three new inpatients every day. The others were treated and allowed to go home. All the children admitted were severely ill and, of that group, one in every twenty died despite our best efforts. In other words, a child's death was a weekly event in the hospital. Almost all of these deaths could have been prevented if we had had more staff and more resources.

I shall never forget what it was like to try to save young lives from the four most dreaded child-killers: pneumonia, diarrhea, malaria, and measles. How we could have just minutes to get enough saline solution into dehydrated children with diarrhea before it was too late. How intensely I hoped that the intramuscular injections of penicillin would be given in time to save young patients with pneumonia.

Even so, my most powerful memories are of the unconscious children suffering from advanced malaria, an illness that in the course of a day can turn a healthy child into a terminally ill patient. Would our injection be enough to save them? They often needed intensive care of the kind we simply could not give them. During the day, a never-diminishing queue of sick children and their relatives snaked across the hospital yard. The hot unshaded space filled up with mothers holding their suffering children, waiting for them to be examined. Often, one glance was enough to grade their state of health: some children were sitting upright while others were utterly limp.

Doña Guita, the only one of our nurses to have six years of

school education and two years of clinical training, sat at the front end of the queue. She was a star. Her task was to place every child into one of two groups: ill but well enough to go to the waiting room, or very seriously ill, in need of a hospital bed and often running a very high temperature. The second group needed immediate treatment and were sent across the yard to the emergency reception.

The mother's eyes often revealed the extent of her worry. When her child was so weary it would no longer breastfeed, a mother's gaze held only desperation and fear of death.

We had thermometers and always recorded temperatures; some children with malaria had a fever of almost 106 degrees, significantly higher than a normal body temperature of 98.6 degrees. I would ask about the breathing and the mother might say, "The breathing is fine, only my child is so hot." I learned the key phrases in Makua. He coughs blood. Tummy hurts very badly.

It was important to look properly at the child. Not being able to make eye contact was a bad sign. I crouched in front of the mother, or sat on a low stool, carrying out the examination while she still held her child. It reassured the mother. I wanted the contact between me and the mother to be as close as possible and asked her only brief, calm questions.

Mostly, the diagnosis was malaria. It could become life-threatening at terrifying speed, but the right medication could turn it round in a few hours. Pneumonia behaved in the same way.

I have a strong memory of one particular late session in the emergency reception room. It was raining outside. A despairing mother held her two-year-old son in her arms. The father, who looked just as sad, stood next to them. The little boy was breathing very quickly, had a low hemoglobin value and was extremely pale. He would not get well unless given a blood transfusion as well as medication. But the hospital did not have a blood bank or any other resources for collecting blood from anonymous donors. When required, we would take blood from a relative with a blood group that was compatible with the patient's.

"But I can't give blood to my child," the father said.

"Why not?" I asked. We were pressed for time.

"Someone in my family might need blood."

I was at a loss. As luck would have it, Mama Rosa, the wise midwife, was standing in the doorway behind me and could explain. Their society was matrilineal and one outcome of this was that the mother's family—usually the mother's brother—was considered responsible for the child. At that point, I found it hard to grasp the strength of this social structure.

"But he has many uncles and I know they will give him blood," the father said.

I freaked out. "Come on, can't I test your blood all the same?"

Mama Rosa explained that arguing was pointless. The father would never accept donating blood to his son. In his eyes, his son belonged to another family, and it was unhealthy to pass blood on to another family. I capitulated.

The father hurried out into the rain. It did not take long before he and two sweating, soaked uncles came running back. One uncle's blood group matched his nephew's. Ten minutes after the transfusion, the child's respiration calmed down and he began to cough. Just a few hours later, the fever started coming down.

Much of what I did at the hospital in Mozambique was actually public health oriented. Ward rounds can be enormously powerful if you talk to the patients in a way that will make them broadcast your ideas when they go back to their villages. In many parts of the world, going to see the doctor provides conversation fodder for weeks.

To me, it had become a matter of my identity: what was I here for? To cure just the patient in front of me, or to improve the health of the whole community?

I decided it was time to work out the right approach by analyzing the matter *numerically*. I would collect data in an interview-based investigation. To make it manageable, I decided to focus on the number of children who died in Nacala city and exclude its rural hinterland. This was because there were three health centers in the city itself and, even if most of the population lived in very meager conditions, most of them could get to one of the centers and be referred to the hospital, or else go straight to the hospital emergency unit if a child was suddenly taken very ill.

That evening spent discussing ethics with my colleague from the regional hospital in Nampula had made me feel this investigation was imperative. I had some rough approximations, using already existing information. The 1980 census showed that Nacala had 85,000 inhabitants and that some 3,000 babies were born every year. A total of 946 children had been hospitalized during the past year and of those, fifty-two had died, despite receiving the best care we could offer them. Almost all of the children admitted to hospital were under five years old.

My next question was how many children under five years of age were dying at home, never making it to hospital? The under-five child-mortality figure for the whole country was 26 percent. The latest census gave us the number of births in the city, roughly 3,000 per year, yet the population of the district was five times that of the city, so we estimated there had probably been five times as many births: 15,000. Twenty-six percent of that number gave us 3,900: the number of child deaths I was responsible for trying to prevent. Despite the fact that one child died every week in the hospital, it was a fraction of the total: I was seeing only 1.3 percent of the children I needed to help.

Talking to the hospital staff, I learned that many children were not brought to the hospital when they fell ill. The main reason was apparently that the families consulted "traditional doctors," who were available round the clock. The alternatives were either one of the town's health centers, open only during the working week, or an emergency hospital admission.

I planned the investigation together with Agneta, who was working locally as a midwife and was also in charge of the childhood vaccination program that we offered regularly in different areas of the town. By then, our friend and colleague Anders Molin was around to share the work with us. Anders had trained in Sweden and been placed in Nacala. Now the town had two doctors, which made a huge difference to us. Anders shared our quarters and became yet another titular uncle for our children. To me, his presence meant an invaluable lightening of my workload.

Our very limited resources meant that the plan had to be very simple. We chose an area of Nacala called Matapuhe, which, according to the census, had a population of 3,700. Next, we arranged meetings with the community leaders and asked for their help in organizing the study.

In the summer of 1981, a group of seven interviewers, all members of our healthcare team, met local women of child-bearing age. The important numbers we wanted were the total number of births and child deaths over the previous twelve months. Most of the women had no schooling at all and did not count time in calendar months, so we used another way of establishing dates: we did the interviews in the holy month of Ramadan, allowing the mothers to recall what had happened in the twelve months since the last Ramadan. We were careful of our manners and how we expressed ourselves when we asked these delicate questions.

It went quickly and well, perhaps especially because, at the same time, we ran a small treatment unit for ordinary health problems and also offered vaccinations for the children. The ready availability of healthcare encouraged participation and attendance. Once I had the data, I extrapolated for the whole town on the assumption that Matapuhe was a relatively representative area.

The outcomes were very clear-cut, beyond any doubts or fuzziness. In one year in Nacala town fifty-two children had died in the hospital and 672 at home: more than ten times as many. An

Hans in Nacala with colleague Anders Molin

arguably even more important observation was that, of those who died at home, about half had not been taken to any care facility in their last week of life. In other words, we had shown a need to organize, support, and supervise local clinics where the staff could manage diarrhea, pneumonia, and malaria before the children became terminally ill. It would save many more lives than giving intravenous fluids to dying children in the hospital.

The child mortality rate in the town turned out to be about 20 percent, not the 10 percent I had originally estimated. We expected it to be higher in the countryside where three-quarters of the region's population lived. I should be trying to prevent more than three thousand child deaths each year, of which only fifty-two were happening in the hospital. It would have been seriously unethical to spend more resources on the hospital before the majority of the population could access some basic form of healthcare.

"Basic healthcare for all" had been a World Health Organization policy since 1978 and the WHO had for decades been prioritizing vaccinations and basic-care facilities for as many children as possible in as many countries as possible. I was lucky to be working in Mozambique, a country that had begun to implement these policies immediately after gaining independence. During my years in Mozambique, many villages were invited to send a representative to the city for a brief period of education. The focus was on creating small healthcare units in all areas, within walking distance for mothers with babies and very young children. They would offer vaccinations and treatments for the main diseases that killed young children.

Were we right to take our lead from the terrible facts of child mortality, rather than to be guided by what was thought to be ethically correct when managing hospital care? Yes. When I was working in Mozambique, child mortality was estimated to be at around 26 percent and, now, thirty-five years later, it is down to

8 percent. It took sixty years in Sweden, from 1860 to 1920, to reduce child mortality from 26 to 8 percent.

During those thirty-five years, Mozambique endured a decade of bloody civil war and coped with a very serious epidemic of HIV. Despite this, its child mortality fell almost twice as fast as Sweden's had almost one hundred years earlier. This also holds true if you compare Europe and Africa overall. Africa is catching up with Europe in matters related to child health, and it is due to accepting evidence-based policies and investment targets.

It can be difficult to persuade oneself to prioritize thinking rather than feeling, but it can be done through careful tallying and thinking clearly about the data.

There was one thing that I still had not grasped through looking at the numbers, though: the true depth of extreme poverty. I understood this first when prompted by the most powerful of feelings—fear.

A whole series of tragic and dramatic events took place during our life in Nacala but we also experienced many good things together. Anders Molin's arrival meant that I could relax when he was on duty and I enjoyed wonderful family Sundays on the beach. As I was no longer on call every night, I could also spend some evenings with the children and sleep soundly at night.

We did the hardest work of our lives in Nacala, but, in the middle of all that, we were a happy family. We grew papaya and kept ducks in the garden, a dry-as-dust patch of sandy soil. Despite the challenges, our health was fine. One magic night, Agneta hugged me and whispered in my ear: "I want another baby." To us, the children were our source of joy and meaning in life. It was how we wanted it to be for many years to come. To me, Agneta's wish sprung from love but also from a shared vision of life beyond my cancer.

She became pregnant faster than we ever imagined and at first her pregnancy progressed well. Together, we followed the growth of her belly by measuring it every Saturday, the day a midwife came to make her own checks. Then, one Saturday toward the end of 1980, we realized that there had been no growth during the past week. There was no change the following week either. We had to take this warning seriously.

During the next week, we had to make a critical decision: would we risk a delivery in Mozambique? No.

In January 1981, Agneta and the children boarded the plane from Maputo to Sweden and I returned alone to Nacala. Our plan was that a month later, just after the birth, I would fly back to be with them.

The day after Agneta and the children had left, there was an outbreak of cholera in our hospital's catchment area. Cholera is fast-moving. Once the diarrhea has set in, a patient can die within a few hours. I immediately gathered a team of three health staff with the necessary equipment and left Nacala. As I had been taught to do, we settled temporarily in the center of the outbreak. Our basic intensive care unit stayed in place for two weeks to do battle with the epidemic in the most distant villages.

One evening, I was stopped on the road by a man who was carrying his unconscious son. The boy was a cholera victim, his sister had already died of the disease and their father knew that he probably would soon lose his second child. At some point after the boy's diarrhea had begun, his father had heard the distant engine sound of our car. He was sure we would come back by the same road and, even though their home was far up in the hills, he had set out for the road, carrying his boy on his back. When he put the child down on the ground, I saw by the glow of the headlights how quickly the sand became wet. The child was losing far too much fluid and must be taken to the unit quickly.

We did not want the cholera infection to soak into the car seat and put him on the floor of the car instead. He was unconscious, his pulse was too faint to detect and there was no chance of making him drink. He was half an hour from death.

The father was completely calm and collected, and entirely focused on his child. Knowing that we had cured other people with cholera, and that his son's fading life depended on me, he was helpful and intensely alert.

It was dark when we arrived at our base unit. We parked the car but kept the headlights on. I asked the driver to shut down the engine so I could hear the boy's breathing. The darkness and silence were broken only by the noise of his breathing and the nighttime sounds of the forest around us—mostly from frogs and geckoes. The father sat still, the nurse stood behind me. Everyone was silent.

I searched for a pulse somewhere. Was he dead already?

Finally, I picked up a faint arterial beat in the groin. I had to get a needle into the big vein lying next to the artery. I sensed the small snap of the needle piercing the wall of the vein. With the needle in place, I could then hook the boy up to an intravenous drip. We had fluid-replacement bags and flow monitors—small chambers showing the flow rate for the drip. The flow began. I crouched in front of the boy with my fingers on his pulse, staring at the monitor, and asked the nurse to let the fluid go in at top speed.

"Hold his legs still," I instructed the father.

He took his son's legs in an iron grip to stop him from moving and damaging the vessel with the needle in it. My body was going stiff from crouching. We were very quiet. The fluid flowed and flowed.

Minutes passed. Five minutes. Ten. Nothing happened. Eleven. Twelve. The boy's eyelids twitched, his eyes opened. He lifted his head. He was waking up.

Still, his father kept himself under control. I heard him behind me, the deep breaths he took as he watched the nurse going down on his haunches to control the boy's first movements. When we had delivered a liter of saline–glucose solution into the boy's blood circulation, I removed the needle and put a plaster over the entry hole in the groin. Then I showed the father how to feed the boy and give him fluids by mouth. He observed me intently while all the time whispering gently to his son.

I thanked the father for his help. He was at a loss and could not think of what to say.

The following morning I went to see them. The boy was better.

Sometimes, our chances of stopping an epidemic depended on curing single cases. My colleague Mama Lucia used to exclaim: "Thank the Lord for cholera." She meant: It makes it so obvious to onlookers that healthcare staff can save lives. Every individual case cured increases trust in doctors and nurses, and so makes public health measures of all kinds more accepted. In order to be believed in by a population you have to create a situation of trust between yourself and the patient's relatives. Returning someone's dying loved one to life after an attack of cholera is an obvious way to instill a sense of respect.

This became very clear to me during a day fighting cholera in another village in a distant rural area toward the end of the epidemic. That day I got a real insight into what extreme poverty means.

We arrived at sunset. Our small, white jeep attracted instant attention. Before we could find somewhere to park, a flock of teenage boys started running alongside us. When I stepped outside, I faced a growing number of people of all ages with their curious faces fixed on us.

The male nurse in our team spoke the local language, Makua. He was about to introduce us when the crowd started to mumble and I picked up two words in Portuguese: *Doctor Comprido*. It was my nickname, based on anatomy: I was the taller of the two Nacala doctors and my colleague Anders had a beard, so we were known respectively as Doctor Tall and Doctor Beard. But it overwhelmed me to find that they had heard of me in this place, one of the district's most remote villages and one I had never visited. I couldn't remember if I had ever treated a patient from here in the hospital. The village was not even within the area covered by our mobile vaccination team.

Instead of introducing us properly, our nurse had to translate my surprised question: "How do you know who I am? I have never been here before."

A man, whose manner indicated that he was the community leader, stepped forward and replied calmly: "You are very well known and respected here. Everyone in this village knows of the doctor in Nacala."

Of course I felt flattered but I was still doubtful.

"I cannot remember treating anyone from here."

The leader knew more than I did.

"Yes, you did. Two months ago, a woman who could not give birth to her child was carried by her relatives to the hospital. You treated her there. Her family and the whole village are all very grateful for what you did for her. That is why you are so well liked here."

No young doctor could fail to be pleased by hearing something like this. I stayed by the jeep, asking about this woman: had her delivery been complicated? Once my question had been translated, the group confirmed by nodding and mumbling seriously if incomprehensibly that, yes, the birth had been very difficult.

After a week of hard and often very frustrating work dealing with cholera, I had no problem with seeing myself as a local celebrity and skilled obstetrician. I looked for a final confirmation from the crowd, which by then had grown to about fifty people. If the birth had been so difficult, were they really satisfied with the care I had given this woman in the hospital? Translation, then smiles, nods and positive mumbling. But my next question, "May I meet this woman?" was followed by a surprising and drawn-out silence. I took this to mean that something had been lost in translation, but the village elder broke the silence with his brief reply:

"No, meeting her is not possible. She died when you tried to get her baby out of her belly." I had never been so astonished and couldn't believe what I was hearing. I repeated the question. The reply, though longer, was in essence the same. When her labor had begun, the baby's arm had come out first., Then the baby had got stuck. The traditional midwives had tried everything they knew about how to get babies out. They had even pulled at the arm until the baby's skin nearly peeled off. At this stage, the woman's husband and her brother decided she must get to hospital, but the village had no means of transport—not even a bicycle.

They made a stretcher from a length of cloth and two long poles, lifted her onto it and carried her twenty kilometers through the forest down to the coastal dirt road, where they eventually managed to stop a passing truck. The stretcher went on the back of the truck and, as dawn broke, they arrived at the hospital.

Doctor Tall had spoken to them on arrival and told them that they had been right: the woman's life was at risk. He had tried to remove the baby, who had died by then, by cutting its body into bits. Then the mother had started to bleed heavily and died. This is why you cannot meet her, they told me.

This terrible story was told to me in translation, sentence by sentence. And now I remembered. I will never forget my pointless efforts to save the life of the febrile, dehydrated woman. It had been another case requiring the extraction of a dismembered baby but this time it was too late. The mother was extremely frail, and already suffering from advanced sepsis after her prolonged labor. Her uterus ruptured from my attempts to extract the dead baby and the hemorrhage killed her almost instantly. It had been unavoidable but I had felt as guilty then as I did now, facing her family and neighbors.

The village headman ended his explanation by expressing again the thanks of the village and how pleased they all were that I had come to be with them. I was by then long past trying to understand why, exactly. My confused brain could only think of one explanation for their satisfaction: they would at last have an opportunity to kill me. I have never gone from pure pride to deepest terror in such a short time. I fell silent and must have looked scared to death.

No one moved. They just kept smiling. I considered asking the driver to leap into the car and drive us away at top speed. But, by then, the car was surrounded on all sides by villagers. Instead, I leaned closer to the bilingual nurse and asked him:

"Do you understand why they say they are so grateful, when the woman died?"

"No, I don't. It's crazy. Shall I ask them?"

I didn't reply, but he put the question to them all the same. People began talking across each other until their leader once more started to speak and they fell silent. His answer was slow and very clearly enunciated but I understood nothing and had to wait for the translation.

"Oh, doctor, we all understand that the situation was very grave and that saving her life was almost impossible. We still are very grateful for everything you did for her. The entire village is grateful because of how you dealt with it, and for that you will be remembered by us."

Now my confusion was complete. I whispered something like "But what did I do?"

The village elder replied in a declamatory voice that was reinforced by the murmured approval of the crowd. To this day, I remember his words as they were translated, sentence by sentence.

"What you did for this woman was very important for her and for her family. It was beyond any expectations of people here, in our remote and extremely poor village. We would never have believed that an important person like a doctor in the big town would do what you did for one of us—a poor woman. After her death, you personally expressed your sorrow to the family. Then, you walked out into the yard in front of the hospital and spoke to the driver of the vaccination van. It was just about to leave but you ordered the driver to wait, and to drive the dead woman's body back home for the burial. You gave the woman's husband a clean sheet so that he could wrap up his wife's body. And you gave him a smaller sheet for the parts of the dead baby. The husband and his brother came home in the van, too. It meant that they all returned home in the afternoon so that, by the evening, the whole family and all the villagers could together give the dead woman and child a dignified funeral. You always remember when you are shown respect during a difficult time. Neither you nor the driver demanded any payment whatsoever. I can tell you now, in all honesty, that her husband and brother between them did not have the money to pay for the transport of their dead. If it had not been for Doctor Tall, they would have been forced to carry their dead all day and night."

Of all the suffering I have witnessed, this particular experience stands out as the most powerful and tangible example of extreme poverty: people are robbed of the most fundamental elements of dignity by sheer lack of money.

A very important aspect of the sad story had however not emerged: I was praised by the villagers for someone else's decisions. Yes, I did have the decency to see the husband and brother after the woman's death and express my deep sadness. But it had not occurred to me that getting the bodies home for burial would be a nearly insurmountable challenge.

After my brief talk with the two bereaved men, someone took hold of my arm and pulled me aside. As so many times before, Mama Rosa wanted a word. She said, quietly and very seriously: "Don't you know that these two men carried her all the way here? It took them the whole night and they have not eaten or slept. Don't you realize that they have no money?"

I hadn't thought of any of this.

"Now, you ought to start thinking about how they are going

to get her dead body home for burial in their distant village." Speechless, I listened to her instructions.

"Go out and stop the vaccination van before it leaves. Tell the driver that he is to take the two men home and also the dead woman and her child. If you don't help them with this, a decade will pass before any other woman from that village seeks help with a difficult pregnancy. Hurry! I can see the van is packed and ready to go."

As has happened so many times in my life, I was given the credit for what other people had done. As I stood there, facing the villagers, I reflected on the boundless reach of Mama Rosa's wisdom.

She had offered them their first contact with a life beyond poverty. For the first time, they had the opportunity to see what healthcare and ambulance services could mean as part of their ordinary lives.

When we had finally controlled the cholera outbreak, I returned to work in Nacala. Soon, the day arrived for me to travel back to Sweden and my family. It was impossible to make international calls from our house in Nacala, and even phoning the capital from the telephone office in the town center was a tricky enterprise. It was only when I disembarked in Maputo that I received news from home. The news was very shocking: our daughter had died a few hours after being born. She had a congenital malformation. Agneta was now in hospital with life-threatening complications following an emergency caesarean.

I boarded a flight to Sweden the following day. At the airport in Paris, I was finally able to speak to Agneta, and later the same day I was sitting by her hospital bed in Uppsala. In the middle of our tragedy and my overwhelming emotions, I remember how impressed I was by the cleanliness of everything in the ward. How the stainless steel tubing of her bed shone. There were no cracks in the floor, the sheets were not torn or patched. The air didn't smell bad. One of the powerful feelings that gripped me as I hugged and kissed Agneta, and wept with her, was my awareness of how lucky we were. Our baby daughter had died but Agneta was alive. If she had given birth in Mozambique, she would have died from the complications that followed her delivery. We could afford to travel and had been born with the correct passports, which gave us the right and privilege to claim treatment from the best healthcare system in the world.

The following day, Agneta was allowed to get up. We drove to the mortuary behind the hospital and spent an hour there with our departed daughter. Then she was cremated and we took her ashes to be buried in the family plot in a cemetery on the edge of the city. Agneta and I went alone, feeling closer to each other than ever. In the hospital, we had been distant from our lives in Mozambique, but standing there in front of our daughter's grave, we felt deeply for the many Mozambican parents who had also lost very young children and whose grief was as profound as ours.

When we returned to Nacala, we noticed a difference in the kind of support we were given. In Sweden, young couples whose children had died were rare. Many of the people around us there seemed to have no grasp of how to approach or comfort us. But in Mozambique, most of our neighbors and colleagues had known similar losses and had traditional ways to offer consolation. We were welcomed back to our jobs in Nacala with both gratitude and great compassion.

4

From Medical Practice to Research

"To: The doctor in Nacala. Come here at once. Over last few days, 30 women and children admitted with paralyzed legs. Query: Polio? Sister Lucia. Health center in Cava."

On an August morning in 1981, I received this note. It had been scribbled on the back of an old cinema ticket. Sister Lucia worked in a small Catholic mission, based in the health center in a remote place called Cava. During my work in Mozambique I had so far only felt the need to apply the basic principles and practices of existing medical knowledge. Sister Lucia's words would change me.

She was a very highly regarded Italian nurse and nun, who for more than twenty years had been working in Cava together with two other nuns. Sister Lucia was well known in the entire region around Cava, admired by the women and respected by the men. Among other things, she was famed for riding a 250cc motorbike and for never asking for help. So I felt her concern must have been prompted by something extraordinary.

The following day, we packed the jeep full of staff, clinical textbooks and equipment. After a day of driving along sandy roads, we arrived at sunset. Sister Lucia stepped outside her office to welcome us, and I noticed straightaway that the Mozambican staff addressed her as "Mama Lucia."

I had assumed that I would start examining patients immediately. Mama Lucia wouldn't hear of it. She took charge, saying that I wouldn't see anyone tonight because it was time to go to sleep. She took us to the simple but clean guestrooms. Mine had a window facing the health center and in the moonlight I could make out the paralyzed women and children sleeping on straw mats spread out on the veranda.

That night, I dreamed of hundreds of paralyzed people.

A knock on the door woke me. We prayed, ate breakfast, and Mama Lucia told us that at exactly 8 a.m. we were to start meeting the patients.

They all told us the same story: suddenly, both their legs had become useless. No pain, no fever and no other symptoms. All of them had fallen ill during the last few weeks, most of them just this past week. They still had sensation in their legs—at least, they could feel me touching different points. Some of them could stand if there was something to lean on but they soon developed spasticity (contraction and spasms) in both legs. This was definitely not polio. But if not polio, then what was it? I could not make my observations fit any disease described in my hefty neurology textbook.

While I continued with my investigations, more afflicted people arrived from villages in the neighborhood. This was feeling more and more strange. Then, an idea struck me: it could be a virus. An infection. That thought triggered another and yet another until thoughts washed over me like waves and I became fearful. Might not I, too, become infected? Or what if I had already caught it—whatever it was?

Fear took my mind hostage. Everything else was put on hold. I tried to check the patients' reflexes but could not concentrate. When I tried to write down what I had observed I had already forgotten and had to start again.

As the afternoon passed, questions crowded into my mind. Why am I stuck here? This wasn't part of the contract. To deal with an emergency of this magnitude, one needs quite different kit from what's available to us. Is it a completely new type of epidemic? Surely there's somebody somewhere who is better equipped to deal with this than me? Somebody who could be flown in?

I had heard that a South African submarine had surfaced in seas near Cava. Had the desperate apartheid regime attacked us with biological weapons? I carried on investigating patients but my dread of my own paralysis, perhaps death, was haranguing me loudly.

"Get out of here!" said my fear. "Report what you have seen and let proper experts take the risks of investigating this."

The intense arguing inside my head was unceasing.

"No, stay. It's your professional duty to collect as much information as possible and to do it now. If this epidemic is to be halted it will depend on what you do today."

And then: "Come on, I'm a foreign doctor. I came here to practice. I didn't sign up to expose myself to unknown, dangerous and probably infectious diseases. Sorry, that's the long and the short of it: I'm not working for a humanitarian organization. I'm a jobbing doctor employed in the region's regular healthcare system. As per my contract."

I struggled to keep my fears under control. In the middle of my ongoing internal debate, which was growing increasingly dramatic, Mama Lucia called me inside for lunch.

"No time for lunch," I replied rudely.

She didn't accept being dismissed, and drew herself up, hands on hips.

"Yes, there is," Mama Lucia said steadily. "You have the time. Whatever else happens here in Cava, at twelve o'clock we meet to pray and eat. If we didn't, we wouldn't have endured for twenty years. How long have you been working in Mozambique?"

"Almost two years," I mumbled.

"So, you're just a beginner. You should do as I say."

Something about her made me obey. Her face had a set, serious expression, She never laughed nor did she ever look tired. Mama Lucia was the boss. I might decide what ought to be done but she would decide *how*.

I pulled off my white coat and washed my hands, as instructed.

By my basin there was a clean towel, soap in a clean dish, and a jug of water. Mama Lucia filled the basin. She always kept order around her.

At twelve o'clock precisely, I sat down at the table to eat lunch with the three nuns. It was soothing to listen to Mama Lucia's long prayer. She was thanking God for my arrival. I did not sense any divine presence but was overcome with respect as I observed the calm of the three nuns—a calm that also began to fill me. At that first lunch with the nuns, I understood the value of taking a break. It is important to have time for contemplation now and then. Perhaps for taking a walk.

During my years in Mozambique I lost weight—I could never get into a balanced rhythm there. Mama Lucia had achieved it though; she was herself, a complete and steady person who appeared free from any doubts about her life's choices. She had decided and now she was content.

The nuns had offered an entire generation of people in and around Cava education and healthcare. They had stayed throughout the long war of independence and kept their place in the world intact during the difficult years after independence. Mama Lucia, who could speak Makua fluently, had gone back home to Italy just once in twenty-one years. And now, even with a nasty epidemic flaring up on their doorstep, the nuns continued their work with dignity and persistence. Some of their thinking was very practical: they had made walking sticks for the paralyzed, for instance.

In the quiet moments while Mama Lucia prayed, my sense of responsibility overcame my fear. I asked myself: who am I, a mere passerby and an atheist who believes in evidence, to get twitchy and want to run away after just two hours? If these women have the staying power to keep going in this place for twenty years, surely I can muster the courage to hang on for two days? Pre-

Mama Lucia (far right)

cisely as she said "Amen," I decided to stay and investigate the outbreak until I had found the cause of this grim disease.

During the next few days, streams of patients, most of them carried by relatives, continued to arrive at the nuns' clinic. When I checked over the summaries of the week-by-week development of the epidemic, my pangs of fear came back: the number of new cases was doubling every week. But it need not be biological warfare. There had been a drought in 1981. People were hungry enough to start eating wild plants. Could the paralysis be due to a combination of poor nutrition and some naturally occurring poison?

I returned to Nacala and discussed the situation with Agneta. Reports of new cases were coming in from more and more villages. We quickly made two decisions. I would have to lead a wide-ranging investigation. My wife and children, on the other hand, were under no obligation to risk contact with a possibly very dangerous virus. They would go to stay with friends in Nampula.

Our agreement gave me a deep sense of satisfaction. If they had stayed, I would have been haunted by unbearable, unceasing anxiety, and work might have been impossible. Agneta explained to the children what a fun time they were going to have and we all helped to pack the car with a month's stay in mind. Agneta told the children to bring their favorite toys and as the car drove away they all waved bye-bye to me. I so admired her calm and felt relieved. Once the car had rounded the corner of our block and driven out of sight, I no longer needed to worry about infecting the children.

In principle, the method for investigating a new form of disease is straightforward. You begin by defining the symptoms so that a brief examination is sufficient to determine whether or not a patient has that particular condition. Our set of symptoms

Patients on crutches in Cava

was uncomplicated: sudden onset of spastic paralysis in both lower limbs and jerking of the leg and foot in response to taps on the tendons below the knee and at the heel. Other obvious tests came out normal: skin sensitivity was unchanged and there were no indications of other neurological deficits, or illnesses such as tuberculosis affecting the spine.

The next step is to include as many people as possible: during the next few weeks, our target was to examine a population of some 500,000 people from our own district and two neighboring ones. Although the area was one of the poorest in the world, we did not anticipate that this would be too difficult. We sought out the elders in the main twenty-five villages and got their agreement to call on the four to five hundred households per village where someone had suffered obvious problems with walking since the last rainy period.

Working out which kinds of walking difficulty fitted our diagnostic criteria was going to be harder. We selected the best nurses who spoke the local language, and taught them how to carry out the neurological tests. They entered the results into a simple form and every night they would run through their cases with one of us doctors. This would eventually enable us to draw a graph of the spread of the epidemic on the map pinned to the wall in our tiny "war office."

The biggest challenge was to estimate the age of the patient and the day of the onset of the illness, because people in these villages lived without calendars. The nurses became accustomed to using the local ways of keeping track of time.

But there was an almost unsurmountable problem: how to find the motorbikes and engine fuel needed to transport the nurses into the countryside and back again. Our region had to turn to the provincial authorities to ask for two cars, and ten or more motorbikes with fuel. We also asked for two doctors, ten nurses, and any available experts on neurology and plant poisons; and for temporary healthcare staff to replace us at the clinic while we investigated the outbreak.

Julie Cliff from the Ministry of Health drove off one evening to hand our request to the head of the province's health service and also to inform the ministry and the World Health Organization in Geneva. Anders Molin and I were left on our own, together with our staff but without any real expectation that the necessary help would arrive any time soon.

I was alone in my office one early morning. Nothing suggested that this room was the headquarters of an emergency investigation into a suspicious outbreak of what might be biological warfare. I was bent almost double over my small, gray-painted metal desk. The floor was covered in brown linoleum. On the sandy road that I could see through the grid in my window, people were streaming past. Most of them were women with young children coming to join the growing queues at the hospital's clinic.

The small hospital in Nacala was located next to a building where the healthcare administration's office was housed. It was a pompous way of describing an office with three people working in one room: Victor, a secretary, and me. Victor had been a typist during the colonial era who since independence had been promoted to administrative head for the local health service.

That morning I had asked Victor and the secretary to write out the forms designed to be the basis of the investigation. We needed hundreds of copies and we of course had no photocopier. Victor figured out that by using one top sheet and three carbon copies you could get four for the price of one.

All the preparations for our study of this ominous epidemic of paralysis were very practical: as well as the forms, we needed wall space for the map of the districts and the graph of outbreaks that we would update daily with case information. I had managed to get hold of some large sheets of cardboard to stick on one of the walls. It was good to have something tangible to do, because I felt profoundly insecure about the whole project. This gave me an opportunity to be on my own and think.

Will this plan work out at all? I wondered. How many weeks or months would it take for the essential motorbikes to be delivered? Victor had told me that there were no motorbikes for sale in the entire province. All the provincial head of the service could do was to commandeer bikes from other districts and give them to us, infuriating their actual owners. Just that morning, I had been explaining the situation to the political district administrator in Nacala. In his opinion, it was a thoroughly bad idea to investigate the epidemic in the way I was suggesting.

"Your staff will simply bring this damned disease into the town. Better to isolate the villages and wait for the whole thing to die down again."

He added that rumors of an epidemic were already spreading and people were becoming frightened. He intended to try convincing the governor of the province, situated in Nampula city, that strong-arm tactics should be used to keep the affected rural areas in isolation. To him, his own political career mattered more than the welfare of the local population.

I was becoming increasingly stressed as I pinned up the sheets of cardboard on the wall. I worried that the young Mozambican republic lacked the kind of wise, strong leaders who would be able to procure enough motorbikes for us.

Yet just a few minutes later, I was proved wrong.

The screech of car brakes outside caught my attention. Once the dust had settled, I saw a truck belonging to the Nacala police, and it was jammed full with motorbikes. Two policemen jumped out and started to unload the bikes. This was incredible. Normally, we had to wait for weeks or months to get a single spare part for just one damaged bike. Then I realized that these were not the white-painted vehicles of the public health service. Our town policemen were unloading all sorts of motorbikes, mostly well worn. Feeling dubious, I went outside to ask how they had managed to find so many bikes in a such a short amount of time. A young policeman shrugged and said:

"The governor issued an order. There's an emergency and you needed motorbikes. Am I right, you wanted ten or so?"

"Yes, I do need them. But how did you get hold of them?"

"Well, the only available motorbikes are the ones on the roads," he said. "We can flag them down. So, we did. We nationalized them, I guess. Governor's orders. We had no choice." The policemen continued unloading the bikes. I could see the Kalashnikovs slung on their backs.

Victor and I had a discussion about what to do next. The Nacala-born Victor recognized the motorbikes and knew who the owners were. We both realized that sooner or later the bikes would be claimed.

It was sooner. Just a brief moment later, the air resounded with desperate cries and shrieks. A group of men came running down the road to the hospital and stopped at the other side of the police truck. It was obvious that they were the owners of the bikes that the police were busy delivering to me. Authoritarian regimes can be efficient but the rulers' rough-and-ready methods tend not to make for harmonious day-to-day life.

I went to stand between the men and their bikes. I began with a calming reassurance.

"You will get your motorbikes back today."

One of the men who spoke good Portuguese asked politely if he might explain to me what had happened. They had been stopped on their way to work by armed policemen who had pointed guns at them. Their motorbikes had been taken and loaded onto the police truck. When the men asked why, they had been told that the doctor needed transport and if they objected, they should talk to the doctor.

The bikes were essential means of work for these men. They constituted their income, their savings, and everything they had.

To have them taken away was huge. Nacala had forty bike owners and we had just robbed a quarter of them.

"You must listen to me now and do as I ask you," I said. "You know that there's an epidemic and it's coming closer."

They had all heard of it.

"I am in charge of stopping it. And the police told the truth: I do need motorbikes, but I didn't know that the police would come and take them away from you. You will get them back today but tomorrow you must come back to the hospital with your bikes. Then you must drive our nurses into the countryside. *You* are the driver of your own bike. The nurse will be riding behind you."

Their greatest fear was to be separated from their motorbike. Once they had understood it wouldn't happen, negotiations could begin.

"What about our jobs?"

I promised that they would be given time off with full pay and asked only to drive their own bikes.

"What about wear and tear?"

"You will be given engine oil."

My non-negotiable point was that the motorbikes must be used to investigate the epidemic. Their non-negotiable point was that no one except the owner would drive the bike and that the owner would take it home with him every night.

The rest of the agreement took two more hours to negotiate. Over the next few weeks, the motorbike owners would come to the hospital office every morning and set out to a distant village with a nurse riding along behind. I would persuade their bosses that these men should keep their wages. The Ministry of Health would give each one of them a liter of engine oil per week to "show appreciation." In the planned economy of Mozambique, engine oil was a hard currency, but it was part of state planning to allocate more oil to the hospitals than we could use. We had an excess of oil, of course, because we never had the state-planned number of vehicles.

By that afternoon, two doctors and a group of newly qualified nurses had arrived by minibus. The following day, the provincial health authority sent us a car. Even in the absence of media hype, any society is frightened by an epidemic outbreak of a serious new disease. During these days in August 1981, we were able to use fear as a lever to get the resources we needed to investigate the situation. There was no help on offer from outside Mozambique—not one dollar, not a single expert. Later, I realized that it had been the minister of health, Dr. Pascoal Mocumbi, who had done everything in his power to provide us with what we needed.

In the villages, elders rounded up everyone showing signs of walking problems. The nurses examined every one of them and a doctor went through their results. Data points began to accumulate on my map- and cardboard-covered office wall. The investigation was under way.

Every established case was entered into the data set. When the nurses returned from their motorbike rides, they came straight to my office to give me an account of their day in front of the graphs and maps. Within six weeks, the large team, with the help of local leaders, had examined half a million individuals and identified a total of 1,102 cases of the paralyzing condition. From the information displayed on the board, two unmistakable patterns emerged.

For each case, we had carefully determined on which day the disease had manifested, so we knew the time profile of the epidemic: it had reached its peak by the end of August, was declining during September and had been reduced to a very few new cases in October.

Geographically, the outbreak was confined to agricultural areas in the interior, around ten to forty kilometers from the coast. There was not a single case in Nacala or the semi-urban district capitals. The afflicted region lay between the fishing communities along the northern coastline and the fertile highlands with higher rainfall. In fact, the outbreak had occurred in an area that normally saw little rain in summer and early autumn and had had none this year. The drought had killed off maize, peanuts, and beans. Only one type of plant had been worth harvesting and it had saved the local people from starvation: cassava, a staple foodstuff in many regions of southern Africa.

It was also gradually becoming clear that gender and age were significant factors. The disease hit children in particular but none under the age of two. Among the adults, the majority of victims were women.

When it comes to investigating an epidemic, collecting and analyzing the numbers is only half of the job. The most urgent task is to establish whether or not the condition is infectious. We went to extreme lengths to locate even one single outbreak in Nacala. I dispatched staff in civvies to pick up suburban gossip and rumors but they couldn't find evidence of even one case. After just three weeks, we were able to conclude that the disease was not transmitted by human-to-human contact, because many people from the disease-ridden areas had visited relatives in town, just as townspeople had gone to stay in the countryside during June, July, and August, yet no one in the town had been affected.

I was becoming more and more certain that we were not dealing with an infectious disease. One evening, I was sitting at the tin desk in my office. The last nurses had returned and made their reports for the day, and the data had been added to the maps and graphs on the wall. We had combed the records of the town's healthcare centers but found nothing.

I gazed at the board-covered wall and suddenly thought: Hans—it's time to stop searching. You have conclusive proof right here. What you see in front of you is incompatible with a disease that spreads from one person to the next. The answer is staring you in the face. The areas with disease outbreaks coincided with the areas stricken by drought. In all probability, the paralysis was caused by malnutrition and some related poison, a combination unique to the people in the outbreak areas.

For me personally, this conclusion mattered greatly. It meant that I ran no risk of becoming paralyzed myself. Emotionally, it felt liberating. That evening, sitting in front of my maps, I wrote a letter to Agneta. I had kept her informed throughout, so I just described how I had arrived at my conclusion. I was quite certain. Once I have thought through an issue properly and worked out my response, I trust it. Now, Agneta and the children could come back home without running the risk of infection.

When my family arrived, we hugged each other for a long time. We slept and ate together, without my harboring the slightest doubt about whether it had been right to bring them home. Work became easier now that I was together with my family once more and able to discuss the investigation with both Agneta and Anders.

We had established that the paralysis was not due to transmission from one human to another but we had still not isolated its cause. This required detective work and I was utterly dedicated to my task. I focused on it to the exclusion of everything else but these were calm, orderly working days. The hospital was run by Anders together with the doctors and nurses we had borrowed from the provincial hospital in Nampula. Systematic, monotonous and madly exciting. No stress. I had time to think. It was fascinating to fill in the data maps and see the overall picture growing clearer and clearer.

Our number one suspect was the drought. The outbreak coincided in time and place with the summer period of no rainfall. As well as analyzing the figures, we traveled to the countryside to find out what people had been eating and how their food intake had differed from previous years.

Their main crop and chief source of food was the bitter type of cassava root. The bitter taste is due to naturally high levels of substances that can form cyanides—just as in bitter almonds. The poison is usually deactivated if the roots are left in the sun for several weeks to dry out slowly. They are then ground into flour to make a thick porridge. The women's knowledge about the detoxification process serves as an invisible lock on the fields and keeps out the three most common kinds of thief—monkeys, wild boar, and hungry men.

It didn't take me long to realize how pointless it was to ask starving people to fill in questionnaires about their eating habits. I had quickly turned into an anthropologist and Agneta helped me in my studies. Gaining the trust of a handful of families and staying with each of them in turn, accompanied by a respectful and kind interpreter, is the most effective way to gain an understanding of personal habits and beliefs.

We heard the same story again and again: "We know the roots are bitter, and in the dry period they became more bitter still. Hoping for rain, we left them in the ground as long as possible to give them time to grow bigger. My husband went to the town to try to get a job and buy some food but then the day came when we had nothing to eat. I pulled up a few cassavas and tried to get rid of the poison by a quick method. I would bash the fresh root to little bits, leave them to dry in the sun for half a day, and then crush them some more. On the second day, I would make flour and prepare some porridge for the children."

Through these conversations, a way of life emerged that none of the patients had mentioned in thousands of medical examinations. We now had insights into the reality of subsistence farming that I would never have fully grasped even after decades of hospital-based work.

We formed trusting relationships with the women because they could offer us the explanations we needed. We needed to know: "What would you do if you had no food at home and no money, and no crops to pull from the fields?"

"I would go to a family that I knew needed help with harvesting. I would sit in the shade of a tree and look down on the ground. They would know what it meant so they would come and ask me if I wanted to help them dig up cassava roots."

One of the women explained that this was a countryside tradition, a kind of social-welfare system rooted in the local culture. The person seeking work would be shown a part of the field where she could harvest all the cassava roots. Her next job was to carry them to the yard in front of the house, peel the roots, and then top and tail them. The middle part had to be halved lengthwise and left in the sun to dry.

Traditionally, she was paid a wage in kind: she could keep the cutoff ends of each root, though if the bits she cut off were too large, she would become known as a "big-end cutter."

"I would never do that. That's a bad name, it shames you. But this year, the difficulty was that hardly any families had enough cassava to let me help them with the harvest."

As I listened to the woman describing this age-old system of assuring food for all, and how it had collapsed, I began to wonder if there could be other factors behind the triggering of the epidemic. But, as so often, it wasn't thinking that led to insights but random observations.

Through my office window back in Nacala, I could see the motorbike drivers arriving back from their day trips to the drought-stricken areas with not only their nurse passengers but also sacks tied to the backs of the bikes. When I asked what was in the sacks, their answers were evasive. Then a nurse told me: the sacks contained sun-dried cassava roots.

"What? You come back from places where there is serious lack of food and the drivers have bought up the cassava from the villages? How can that be?" I demanded.

This was obviously a sensitive matter, but one of the nurses stood up for the drivers.

"They are paying good prices. You can't imagine how expensive cassava flour is in town nowadays. It's because of all these months of drought."

This was an example of centralized planning at its worst. The socialist government had forbidden private trade in food but had failed to satisfy the needs of the people from centrally held stocks. A black market for cassava had grown up and was swallowing both official and unofficial supplies.

We drove out to a village that had been badly hit by the paralysis and tried to find out if the families were selling cassava on the black market rather than helping their neighbors.

This was a delicate matter because such trade was forbidden. After spending the day with some of the families as they worked in the fields, we had built up good relationships. But every time I tried to shift the talk to cassava sales, they avoided the subject. Finally, we had to leave. As we walked to the car, the male head of one of the households took my hand and pulled me aside. This had happened many times before—many crucial pieces of information came my way just as I was about to leave, sometimes when we hugged good-bye.

The man looked me in the eye and said: "We understand what it is you want to know, Doctor. You know as much as we can tell you. It's a family secret if we have sold cassava or not. We will never speak of this with anyone."

What he said revealed that they had sold every root they could lay their hands on. None of them would ever admit it, for two reasons: it would be a breach of the Marxist government's doctrines and, worse, it would be a breach of the rules of local culture.

Finally, the rains came and there were no new cases of paralysis. We carefully wrote up the data and our preliminary conclusion: that the nerve damage had been the result of a combination of undernourishment and an unusually high intake of a naturally occurring toxin. The underlying causes were the drought and probably a lack of alternative ways of getting food during periods of scarcity.

We presented our five-page report to Dr. Pascoal Mocumbi, the minister of health. Wanting to understand better, he quizzed us. Then he thanked us for our work and presented us with a signed copy of a book about Mozambique.

There is something deceptive about the battle against epidemics. You are duly praised for the immediate, dramatic actions. But it is building and managing a better community that saves the greatest number of lives; the steady, unrelenting work that goes into this rarely receives the attention it deserves.

This epidemic had taken me into local villages and households, closer to individuals. Through them, I accumulated insights into people's ways of life and could observe with my own eyes how a system could break down and stop functioning. Later, I would study such collapsed systems in order to better understand the various components that must be functional if a society is to haul itself out of extreme poverty.

All this happened as our contract in Nacala was reaching its end. We had undertaken to work there for two years and these years were nearly up. We had endured, and we had completed our tasks.

By then, I was exhausted and the rest of the family was very tired too. Still, we had not hit a wall and given up—we had broken through it. I had survived cancer; our newborn child had died; we had fought an epidemic; we had gained a hard-won intellectual grasp of how hard it is to develop a country and how long it takes. At that point, despite all the questions the epidemic had raised and left still unanswered, it did not occur to me that I would return home only to spend the next twenty years researching just these questions.

The one thought dominating all our minds was that we were going home to rest.

As planned, we had packed up our work and our home by the end of October 1981. We were happy, despite the challenges we'd faced, and tightly united as a family. But if someone had asked me to stay for one more week, I would have burst into tears.

We had promised Anna and Ola—now aged seven and five—a little holiday before going home. We realized there would be no time to rest in Mozambique and decided to take a break on our journey home to Sweden, which took us via Geneva. We had to go there anyway to hand in blood and urine samples from our investigation into the epidemic for analysis at the WHO's toxicology department. Mozambique lacked the necessary technical resources.

We rented a car in Geneva and marveled at the experience of driving such a clean, perfectly functioning vehicle. There were child seats in the back and Agneta sat next to me in the passenger seat. We looked at each other. I turned the key and suddenly classical music streamed from the loudspeaker. The sensation was dizzying. We had landed on "another planet" and I could barely take it all in.

Our samples were in a large freezer box in the back of our spotlessly clean rental car. They were kept cold with dry ice but we knew the CO_2 would soon evaporate, so we were keen to hand them over. It brought an enormous sense of relief to transfer responsibility by leaving the samples in a fridge in the basement. We left the massive WHO building feeling content.

What to do next? We turned to our children and it struck us how tattered they looked. Everyone in Geneva was nicely dressed, except us. Our children looked as though they'd been dressed in bits and pieces from a flea market, even though we had tried to dress them up for the journey.

So, we went to a big shop to buy clothes for the children. That same evening, they wrote their lists of Christmas wishes to hand over to their grandparents when they came to meet us at Stockholm Arlanda Airport.

Readjusting was a quick process, and the children made a real effort at it. We bought them satchels for school. Everyone got an appointment with the dentist. Agneta returned to her job at the maternity unit and I to mine in the medical wards. We really were very shocked to see how different everything was in Sweden. We had new winter tires fitted on our shabby little blue car and we booked a slot with a photographer for Christmas card photos. We immersed ourselves back into Swedish family life.

But after a while, leftover tasks from Mozambique began to pop up in our thoughts. Agneta had promised to edit a booklet with instructions for maternal healthcare and family planning. The text was ready and we had it printed and shipped to Maputo.

I had received a letter from Maputo telling me that so far, no analyses had been made on the samples I had left in Geneva. My friend and colleague Anders Molin, who was also back in Sweden, said he was worried that the paralysis epidemic would strike again in the next dry season. It had been easy to adjust to life at home but it also proved impossible for me to forget the experiences from Nacala and the responsibilities I still bore.

Was the form of paralysis I had observed truly a condition new to medical science?

One morning in spring 1982 I was given a push to carry on with this line of research: a seriously mobility-impaired patient came to see me at my clinic in Hudiksvall. Her entrance into my office stunned me so completely I forgot to greet her: she walked with crutches, her knees turning inward and her wrists twitching at every step. It was exactly the same spastic pattern that I had been investigating a few months earlier in Mozambique. She told me that it was an inherited disease. She had been an adult when the first signs appeared and her difficulties had grown worse with time. She wanted to know if there was a way of stopping further deterioration. She had been seen by a specialist a few years earlier but had been offered no treatment.

"Has there been any new research that could help me?" she asked.

After examining her, I promised that I would search for a way of halting the progress of her condition but that it would take a couple of weeks. I would contact her and arrange another appointment.

Later that day, I knocked on the head consultant's door eager to talk to him. Pontus Wiklund knew his town very well and would be able to identify the family with this heritable health problem. He listened and looked curious.

"You see," I said, "it looks precisely like the nervous deficit we saw in the paralysis cases I investigated in Mozambique. If it's inherited, I must read all the literature there is. Any more information would help us arrive at a better understanding of the underlying cause."

My wise boss smiled and said he had always thought I would end up in research. It was fortuitous that I had presented my ideas just this week: health service research funding for doctors was in the pipeline and he had been feeling ashamed that no one from his department had put forward an application. I applied and was duly given a grant to study the links between the epidemic of lower limb paralysis in Mozambique and the cases of similar, inherited paralysis in Hudiksvall. All this brought on a crisis of identity. I was a reluctant researcher.

I had always suspected there was something phony about research and didn't much care for it. The terminology sounded pretentious and the format of what you said seemed to matter more than the content. I was irritated by the stagey, vaguely pompous ceremony surrounding things like the presentation of degrees. Generally, I was skeptical about the whole elaborate system and found it hard to shift out of my underdog perspective. All these attitudes I would later dismiss as silly. For one thing, academic events are important for networking with colleagues and other contacts.

I sought advice from senior academics: what should I do next? Their suggestions were straightforward: go on research leave for a couple of months and read everything you can find about the conditions you are interested in. Apply for funding to follow up your earlier work on-site in Mozambique. Meanwhile, try to land a post at Uppsala University Hospital so that you become a member of an academic organization. And register your doctorate now: you need to learn more about how to do research.

I wrote up a plan for my doctoral thesis and it was accepted. It was my good fortune that my supervisor was Bo Sörbo. He was a tall, kind man who had spent a large part of his life on toxicology research, driven only by his own curiosity and not by a taste for titles and status. He taught me what science is really about.

Bo Sörbo had an absolutely decisive influence on my career. Apart from being a brilliant chemist, he was also an easygoing person, a family man and a football enthusiast. At the outset, I worried about having to write an entire doctoral thesis, but Bo told me to relax.

"Never mind the academic formalities, just get on with the work. The actual research is going to take many, many years," he said.

However, he was quick enough when it came to getting results. Two days after I had delivered the samples from the Mozambican patients to him he was on the phone to me, speaking excitedly.

"You were right! The people who were sampled had been ingesting something that gets broken down into cyanide in the body. You must apply for more money to go back and conduct a follow-up study!"

Over the next two years, I went back to Mozambique for several short periods of fieldwork, bringing home samples to be analyzed in Bo Sörbo's laboratory. I read as many research papers as I could find and wrote five papers based on my own work.

Meanwhile, my family grew, with the wonderful addition of our son Magnus, who was born in 1984. After another spell of parental leave, I compiled my research results into a thesis, which I presented in 1986.

My results had come out in support of my preliminary conclusions from 1981. The drought had killed off all other cultivated plants except for cassava, and cassava production had been low compared to normal levels. The food shortages made people resort to leaving the roots to dry in the sun for a shorter time than usual, which meant that they contained far more than usual of the substances that could be metabolized into cyanide. I wrote about the new condition using technical, descriptive terms but discovered that it already had a name. In the 1930s, an Italian doctor working in the Congo had written a report on an identical outbreak of paralysis. The local people called it *konzo*, which meant "bound legs" in their language.

By now, you will have an idea of who I was in 1986: a proud young father of three children, and a qualified medical man with an academic doctorate. I had not only described a disease but could also claim that my research had identified a possible cause for it. I remember being both baffled and miffed when other university scientists seemed rather less impressed than I had anticipated. I was probably not especially easy to get along with at the time. Anyway, I had been focused on work and now it was time to take a long summer break with my family.

We had decided to rent a house for the summer on an island in the Stockholm archipelago. It was the very best kind of family summer holiday. We were free. Agneta had just completed two years of the medical curriculum. I had been cancer-free for eight years and began to feel that I must be cured. My professional future looked promising and full of new opportunities.

On my first day back at the university after the holiday, I received a shock as deeply felt as any unpleasant surprise can be by a young scientist who thinks too well of himself. This was the final sentence in a new paper on konzo and it spurred me on to continue with my study of the illness for another fifteen years:

> Our observations indicate that the cause is an infection and therefore does not support an explanation based on cyanide poisoning due to substances present in local foods, a hypothesis put forward to account for an outbreak of a very similar disease in Mozambique.

With mixed feelings of anger, curiosity, and duty, I settled down at once to study the article. I read it several times, from beginning to end. It was written by scientists from Belgium and the Democratic Republic of the Congo, or Zaire, as it was known then, and published in a leading neurological journal.

Their paper stated that they had come to three important conclusions. The first was that konzo outbreaks still occurred in the Congolese region of Bandundu. The second was that konzo and the condition I had investigated in Mozambique were the same disease. So far, so acceptable for the tense reader. Their third major finding upset me, though: their statement that konzo was, in all probability, caused by a viral infection. They went on to suggest that I had been wrong to conclude that the cause was a combination of malnutrition and ingestion of cyanide precursors present in cassava.

In my view, their interviews with families had been handled in too cursory a way. However, with every new read-through, I grew steadily more humble. I slowly realized that my wise supervisor had been right to say that a doctoral thesis was simply a driver's license that allowed the graduate to gain more experience in research. I also realized that I would not be able to counter their evidence from where I currently sat. I was going to have to investigate the situation in remote parts of the Bandundu region. Over the following days, I sought out my academic mentors and listened to their advice about how to best handle what I called "the attack from Belgium."

My distinguished advisors offered their opinions clearly. First, nothing would be gained by starting an argument. The conclusion that we were dealing with an infectious disease was reasonable. However they agreed with my reasoning that my critics' interviews with the afflicted families in Congo about their cassava consumption had been quite superficial. Also, the researchers had not analyzed any blood samples.

"Hans, you've got to go to the Congo and interview people properly," Bo Sörbo said, nearly shouting. "And bring samples back for analysis!"

He was wildly excited by the notion that I would be bringing blood samples from remote parts of Africa back to his lab in Linköping.

"But I've no money to do it," I replied wearily.

"Then you must apply for new grants! It's in your favor that somebody has published a paper saying that you're wrong. It will increase your chances of getting the funding you need."

I understood well enough. Bo Sörbo was right. I had to go to the Congo.

The preparations took two years. I had to write official letters to ministers and my university for permissions to do the studies and I had to ship equipment to the capital, Kinshasa (first it was mistakenly sent to Kingston, Jamaica and had to be dispatched back across the Atlantic). More importantly, I had to establish a network of contacts in the region's villages.

I was assisted by my local colleague Banea Mayamba, a young Congolese doctor and postgraduate student, who was also the head of the local authority dealing with food and nutrition. He claimed that as he came from a tropical region he was incapable of orderly thought in temperatures below 75 degrees and had arranged it so that it was always at least 82.4 degrees in his office.

There was a tradition at our university that was supposed to make the postgraduate students feel more confident that they were making progress: they were encouraged to nail their thesis to the wall. Actually, the idea was to hammer a nail into the wall, punch a hole in the corner of their "book," thread a loop of string through it and then hang it up. Seeing it there on the wall was supposed to raise the self-belief of students scared to death by the thought of the public viva examination. Banea had never learned how to hammer a nail into anything so I took a board into work and made him practice in the secretary's office on the day his thesis came back from the printers.

Banea and I built a chain of trusted contacts, first between Uppsala in Sweden and Kinshasa in the Congo, then between Kinshasa and the small town of Masi-Manimba, and from there to the clinics and the nuns in the Catholic mission in Lumbi. Finally, and crucially, we had to talk to the village elders who, in turn, would try to convince local people to take part in our study. We needed everyone to understand exactly what we proposed to do, and why, and to give their consent to being involved. Previous studies had shown me the hard way that nothing could be done if people considered you to be a complete stranger.

I brought a postgraduate student with me from Sweden, a man called Thorkild Tylleskär. He had entered my life a few years earlier, during a lecture I gave on the medical course in Uppsala, during the so-called disaster medicine week. Thorkild asked detailed questions about cassava cultivation, with an intensity that ignored any conventions of politeness. He spoke eagerly, leaning forward as if to get closer to the answers, and smiling all the time. He was curious, argumentative, and uninhibited. I would later discover he was also possessed of a special capacity for absorbing details and very hardworking.

Thorkild had taken a break from his medical studies to take a course in African languages at the Sorbonne. During an earlier visit to northern Congo he had learned from the Baptist Church missionaries there that they did not address the local people in

On board a boat in the Congo

their local language, Sakata. As Thorkild and his wife planned to work as missionaries, after the course they had headed off to a Congolese village where they lived for a year while he charted the structure of Sakata and finally wrote it up as a master's thesis in African linguistics. After all that, he had returned to his medical studies. Now, he was coming with me to investigate konzo in one of the agricultural areas of the Congo.

Our first night was spent in the capital. Before leaving for the countryside, I was nervous and could not sleep. After two years of preparation, we could not afford any failures. I turned on the light several times to add another item to my to-do list and run through again the details of our plans for each day, though I was well aware that most of our plans would be subject to abrupt changes due to unforeseen circumstances.

When I finally accepted that I could do no more that night to prevent the project from going wrong, I tried to sleep but was assailed by new worries. What about my own safety? The chief danger was car accidents; driving at night was out of the question. What about illnesses? I had taken my malaria tablets and had all the necessary vaccinations. My personal medical kit included the most effective antibiotics available. But there were risks that medical precautions could not deal with, in particular robberies and other forms of violence. What if we were met with aggression? I had experience in approaching people respectfully in remote farming areas, being polite and taking the time to listen. Talking with both leaders and ordinary people was essential before trying to do anything at all—it was a rule I intended to follow. Permission from the authorities was a formality but what really mattered was that every local leader and every member of the studied population knew our reasons for being there and agreed to our conditions.

Before I finally fell asleep, I thought about my wife and my children. Earlier that evening, I had been on the phone to Agneta but, from tomorrow, we would not be able to contact each other for three weeks—mobile phones did not yet exist and where we were going there were simply no telephone lines. My family would be in complete ignorance of my whereabouts. Once my worrying about the research program had faded into worry about my own safety and then into feelings of guilt and concern for my family, I finally fell asleep.

The following morning, we left Kinshasa. We were a team of about ten people and traveled in two heavily laden jeeps.

As we drove through the outskirts of Kinshasa, a city with several million inhabitants, the communities looked more and more impoverished. The conventionally built-up center of the city was ringed with densely populated slums where living conditions were grim. We were driving east toward the rising sun on a two-thousand-kilometer-long road that crossed the entire country. The heavy traffic, consisting mainly of trucks, was dangerous because the tarmacked lanes of the road were so narrow. At first, we could get glimpses of the Congo River but then the road turned away and took us up onto the high plateau. We were on our way.

The tarmac was riddled with potholes, which kept our speed well down. We took our first break in the small town of Kenge. A row of packed stalls lined the sandy road into town—everything a traveler might need was on sale there, including local produce like bananas and peanuts, and car parts, T-shirts and shorts. A tailor was on hand to mend torn clothes. Most of the travelers were poor so the goods on sale had to be cheap. Many traveled standing on the back of a truck, squashed in with thirty or so others. They had to carry water cans because of the exposure to heat and strong sunshine.

The farther east we went, the clearer it became to me that we were entering a world of extreme poverty. The road lost definition and became a shapeless, sandy piece of ground. Nothing shows more explicitly and more cruelly how poor people are than the dangers they are prepared to face in order to travel to places they need to go. On the Congolese roads, journeys were full of risks. The relatively flat savannah landscape is crossed by deep valleys. The flat ground invited drivers to speed, while the old, badly-maintained cars ran into trouble in the valleys, often because of faulty brakes.

Old car wrecks along the road were warning signs. A terrible accident had taken place along one stretch we passed. A truck was upside down and, on the grassy roadside, six corpses had been covered by sheets. The rescue work seemed to be directed by men with red crosses on their jackets. We pulled up alongside to find out if anyone required medical help. We learned that the truck, loaded with thirty passengers, had driven down into the valley at speed. On the downward slope, the driver had moved the gears into neutral to save fuel. The truck had careered across the bridge and started up the other side but the driver couldn't get the gears to re-engage and it lost momentum. As the truck began to roll backward, the driver jumped out through the window and disappeared. The driverless vehicle missed the bridge and fell into the river. Some of the injured had already been taken to the hospital, six dead passengers had been hauled out of the water and many more were still missing. Since there was no more we could do, we headed on our way.

The volunteers told us that unless some relatives came to identify the dead and take them away, the corpses would be buried next to the road. In a society without the resources to maintain decent roads and vehicles and provide sufficient traffic police, people have to work out their own ways of dealing with road-traffic accidents and the injured or dead victims.

Just before sunset, we reached Masi-Manimba, a small town in the highlands, around six hundred meters above sea level. Most of the houses were simple dwellings with walls made of dry mud. The name of the town recalled the African sleeping sickness: Masi-Manimba means literally "the place where people sleep" in the Kikongo language.

During the colonial period, teams sent out to identify the parasite that caused sleeping sickness had collected blood samples from local people. The village elders told us this when we met up with them the following day. They added that each of the village blood donors had been given a tin of sardines by the technicians.

"It's a serious matter, drawing blood from poor, hungry people. You must explain carefully why you're doing this. And you need to bring nuns along to help. They return to villages year after year and are respected everywhere," advised the head of the local health service.

We said that we were very aware of this and that we were going to stay with the nuns in Lumbi. The mission had been set up by the Sisters of the Cross and Passion and the five nuns there, all of different nationalities, were known as "the passionate sisters." Their small collective was to be our base for the next few weeks.

The abbess was a wise, cautious woman. She agreed to let one of the young nuns join our scientific team. Sister Kalunga was Congolese, knew the local language and had just completed her nursing qualification. Her presence would strengthen what I thought of as the "chain of trust."

Toward the evening of that day, we set out to drive to the mission. The road was so poor it took us an hour to cover just twenty-five kilometers. The nuns gave us a warm welcome and showed us to the guest rooms.

Then we had several meetings with the nuns to explain and discuss our research. We also decided that a local schoolteacher who spoke French as well as the region's indigenous languages would accompany us to the villages. Her presence completed our chain of trust. The teacher's loyalty and translation skills would later save my life.

The nuns ran a well-organized hostel. In the evening we dined at a long table beautifully laid with a tablecloth, napkins, and jugs of iced water. Dessert was served after the main course and with it liqueur glasses were set out. The next moment, I spotted

Sister Linda step into the room, smiling happily and holding a large bottle in her hands. I realized that this could become problematic. My Swedish colleague Thorkild was a Baptist and, as an active member of the church, would not drink alcohol.

Sister Linda's bottle turned out to contain homemade orange liqueur. Thorkild began to say something in his fluent French about not wanting any of the drink. The nun looked troubled and I intervened quickly, holding out my glass to show how keen I was to be served and simultaneously elbowing Thorkild in the midriff, whispering "Come on, it's about culture—not religion. You had better drink the stuff and smile to show how much you appreciate these wonderful nuns."

Thorkild drank, smiled and chatted pleasantly with Sister Linda. She seemed to enjoy his many questions about making liqueur. What's the method? How much sugar do you use?

It mattered enormously to me that the nuns understood how grateful we were for all their efforts. These women were essential for our continued work.

(Later, Thorkild got his revenge when we were eating with the villagers after a day of interviewing in a remote place on the savannah. Supper was fried rat. Thorkild whispered: "It's all about culture, you know. You'd better eat this fried rat and show how much you appreciate these wonderful hosts." I ate the rat meat with a smile. We got on just as well with the villagers as with the nuns.)

Work began the next day. We divided the team to cover visits to twenty-two villages in the neighborhood. All were within a radius of about ten kilometers and could be reached by narrow lanes, sometimes only on foot. The first task was to introduce ourselves and our research program to the elders and the other villagers. When—and if—they accepted us, we would count the inhabitants and examine everyone with walking problems to find out who suffered from konzo. The most densely populated and most distant of the villages was a place called Makanga and it was

At work in the Congo

said to be particularly afflicted by konzo, with many paralyzed children. There, we were also to interview people about their diet and take blood samples.

It was my job to go there.

We set out in the jeep the next morning: Banea, the nurses, the teacher who would interpret, and me. It took us an hour. The narrow roads, sometimes just paths, crossed stretches of savannah and climbed up ridges with views over river valleys and deep clefts covered in rain forests. People were growing cassava on the dry savannah as well as on the slopes of the hills. They used whatever construction materials they could find for their homes: walls were made of sundried mud, and floors of flat-trodden soil, while roofs were covered with grass. Hardly any of the houses had doors.

When the jeep rolled into Makanga, we were greeted by barefoot, thin children in worn clothes, who came running alongside us, full of charming curiosity.

We spotted at once that some of the children were limping, with the characteristic spastic leg movements of konzo.

The village elder lived in a house at one end of the village and we pulled up outside it. He knew we were coming and had chairs for us arranged in a circle in the shade of a nearby tree. Some men, who seemed to be the elder's advisors, chased the eager children away and then sat down on the ground nearby. We talked for an hour—an agreeable conversation. We described our plans and he asked us many questions about them. We waited until the elder's questions had been answered, and finally we made a deal. Our interviewers would count the houses in the village, draw up lists of the size of each household and start examining everyone who had problems with walking. The elder agreed to our taking blood samples, provided all sampled people were given a tin of sardines, as they had been whenever samples had been taken during the colonial occupation. However, he and his advisors considered it unnecessary to bring everyone together for a collective explanation followed by a question-and-answer session.

"This village is too large for that kind of thing. They'll do what we've agreed here. I'll come with you. They trust me," the elder said with a smile that turned into a laugh.

We also asked to rent an empty house where the blood samples would be taken and where we could keep our small diesel generator and the centrifuge machine we needed to separate the blood. We wanted to keep the curious—children and adults—at a certain distance.

I insisted that we should talk to the families who gave blood samples, even though I had accepted that we could start the counting without first arranging a big meeting for everyone. I checked with the interpreter that my point had been clearly translated and understood. The elder agreed and said that this could be done the following day outside our makeshift laboratory. We also followed our usual practice of employing two local teenagers, a boy and a girl, to help with the work in the lab. It was a good way of creating a wider understanding of what we were up to and, besides, visitors offering job opportunities are always popular. In addition to their modest wages, the two young people would be given a certificate stating that they had participated in a research project.

We had spent time thinking through the details of the visits and we were relaxed about the pace of things. There should, we felt, be plenty of time for discussion, which required more time because everything had to be translated. Most of the villagers spoke several languages, but they communicated with strangers in Kikongo, the lingua franca of the southern Congo, rather than in French.

The first day was free of trouble, and we were accompanied around the village by the elder, as agreed. He asked people, apparently very kindly, to tell us how many people lived in each house and who had problems walking. I noticed that from time to time his voice became quite harsh, but no one seemed to protest. When we had finished the count, we inspected the building that would become our laboratory, a small structure with a straw roof and walls made of mud bricks. I chatted with the two teenagers who had been picked by the village elder to assist us. Once our tasks for that day were done, we drove back and returned to the nuns at sunset. They were waiting for us and had prepared another splendid dinner, with a glass of orange liqueur. Before doing anything else, we walked down to the river and washed off the dust of a day on the roads and in the village. The mission guest rooms were very clean but had no running water.

The following morning, we loaded the jeep with a small diesel generator to power the centrifuge machine. The blood samples had to be spun so that they would separate into parts, and then stored in large steel thermos flasks. All this equipment looked interesting to the locals—nothing like it had ever been seen in the village before. When we had parked the jeep and started unloading, people came along to have a look. Our two local assistants turned out to be very useful. Their first task was to explain to the crowd what we were doing. At the same time the interpreter and I and our two assistants started to set up the equipment. Banea walked off to prepare for the interviews. I was feeling upbeat as I began. The hut had been cleared and cleaned as I had requested. There I was, installing essential equipment for the research project we had been planning for two years. It was satisfying. I started up the generator and tested the centrifuge. It made quite a lot of noise and, for a few minutes, I could not hear what was going on outside.

When I shut the centrifuge down, I picked up the sound of angry voices. My mood changed in a few seconds. I crouched down to get out through the low doorway and when I straightened up again, I realized that the whole area around the lab hut was full of people who sounded very upset indeed. They must have seen how frightened I was. Suddenly, their voices became louder and along with the many fingers pointed at me, two men raised machetes and waved them about in a very threatening manner. The man closest to me seemed especially ill-tempered. The arm holding the machete had a scar running all along it. I was as scared of machetes as of guns. As a medic in Mozambique, I had cared for several patients with grave injuries inflicted by these weapons. One woman had had her face slashed from ear to ear at a level just below her eyes. The cut had severed the tip of her nose and exposed her nasal cavities. I had spent an entire afternoon stanching the hemorrhage.

My one hope was the crowd of people separating me from the machete-waving men. During this panicky moment, the only familiar face I could see was the interpreter's. He had come to stand next to me in the doorway. Loyalty had made him join me as the crowd grew.

More and more people were arriving. The interpreter leaned closer to me and whispered, "The others have left." He meant the rest of the research team, and sounded very frightened.

"I think we should run," he said. "They are very angry." In just a second, my fear intensified sharply. I grabbed the interpreter's wrist and held on to it.

Two thoughts went through my mind.

The first was that without the interpreter I would be lost, because it was only through him that I could communicate. The second was the memory of what I had been taught by the provincial governor in Tanzania, after another, rather less dramatic, confrontation with a man brandishing a machete. The man had become furious with me because I had taken a photo of his wife without asking him first. I had solved that conflict by holding out the camera in my hands, palms up, when he ran at me with his weapon.

"You did the right thing," the governor said afterward. "Never turn your back to an angry person who is threatening you with a machete. He is ten times more likely to try to cut you down if you run away."

I glanced left and right for an escape route. Not a hope. If the people wanted to hurt me badly there were more than enough of them to hold me down and let the man with the machete have a go. My only choice was to talk myself out of this.

Fearful, I raised my arms and almost whispered: "Wait. *Attendez. Attendez.*"

The teacher translated. Without letting go of his wrist I managed to get a grip on a wooden box standing just inside the door and turn it upside down. Then I stood on it. My fear drove my mind to form a few sentences in French.

"I'll leave at once if you don't want me here. But I can explain why I am here."

"Tell us, tell us!" a majority called out, clearly not so outraged that they could not wait for a bit.

"I have come to find out why your children cannot walk anymore."

"You have come to steal our blood!" a voice shouted.

Slowly, I carried on explaining. I had studied the same illness in Mozambique and Tanzania. They were not impressed. I said something about drying the cassava root for too short a time, but most of them protested.

Suddenly, after perhaps only a minute or two, a middle-aged woman stepped forward. She walked straight to me where I stood, perched on the box. Exactly in front of me, she turned to face the crowd. She raised her arms in an eye-catching gesture and addressed her neighbors in a loud voice:

"Do you remember when our children were dying like flies because they had measles?" She continued: "Then, they brought the vaccine, and ever since, the nurses vaccinate our newborn babies, and our children no longer catch measles and die."

She paused for dramatic effect and took a step forward.

"How do you think they knew about the vaccine? Where did they find it? Do you think vaccines grow in the trees of faraway countries? No, of course not. They understood how to go about making the vaccine because of what this doctor calls research."

She spoke in a measured tone, one sentence at a time. And as she uttered the word "research," she turned round to point at me. Then she looked back out over the crowd where the two men with machetes stood waiting.

"The doctor says that he and the two Congolese doctors are here to find out why so many women and children in our village lose the ability to walk because of the illness we call konzo. He does not claim to be able to cure it here and now. But if it is possible to find out why so many of us are stricken, perhaps we can get rid of konzo just as we got rid of measles. It makes sense. Here in Makanga, we need this research."

She turned her back to the villagers, took a step toward me and reached out her arm. She pointed with her other hand at the inside of her elbow and exclaimed: "Doctor, take some of my blood!"

Her speech had taken little more than a minute but the effect was startling. The men stopped waving their machetes about. Expressions changed from fury to smiling recognition. Shouting was replaced with gentle voices as people started to queue up behind the woman. While most of them joined the queue quickly, a few walked off with the machete-wielders.

I remember exactly what was said back then, in a small, isolated Congolese village. Twenty-eight years have passed since that day but I can still recall the woman's address as sentence by sentence, she transformed the crowd's fear and aggression into sympathy and understanding.

I will never forget how she saved my life.

The rumors that we visitors had sinister reasons for collecting blood had spread like wildfire. In less than an hour, they had stirred up fear and fury. This was because of an ancient notion that you could be harmed by having some of your blood taken from you. It was not surprising that this misunderstanding should exist in an isolated village in the Congo. I had dreaded incidents like these, which I knew could happen if any link broke in the chain of trust.

It wasn't just the woman's insight that saved me from death by machete, but the way she expressed the logic behind her argument. She changed her fellow villagers' way of thinking so that they could see that their fears were the outcome of hasty, emotional responses.

Over two decades of visiting distant places, I would meet other women like her. They would tell me how much they hated their poverty, and how they dreamed of education and decent health-care for their children. And a nice, comfy foam-rubber mattress to sleep on. It was my memories of these women that would later make me confront the opinions of my Swedish students who argued that the poor were happy with their lot and should carry on being poor—"They mustn't live the way we do, it would ruin our planet."

For many years, I continued to spend around a month annually conducting field studies in small, remote communities in the Congo and other African countries. Together with graduate students and postdoctoral colleagues, I published a long series of scientific papers and, eventually, the disease we had described became a standard entry in neurology textbooks. We also developed new analytical methods and even had patients flown to Sweden for advanced neurological examinations. Our observations confirmed the hypothesis that konzo symptoms follow the sudden decay and death of nerve cells that conduct signals from the brain to the musculature of the lower limbs. The condition occurs only among extremely poor people living in isolated communities, who become wholly dependent on cassava as a basic foodstuff. It strikes individuals who have existed on a diet of badly prepared—and therefore poisonous—cassava roots for some four to six weeks. Regrettably, the nerve damage is permanent, but the paralyzed person can be to some extent rehabilitated by using lightweight crutches.

Despite these findings, I was gradually losing interest in the medical, toxicological, and biochemical aspects of the disease. Instead, I was keen to look into the underlying causation. The agricultural economy was driving a vicious circle of deprivation and extreme poverty.

5

From Research to Teaching

The roll call had been done. My first lecture was due to begin. During the lunch break, I had smuggled the small blanket into a drawer in the teacher's desk. No one knew it was there.

My job was to tell around thirty trainee doctors and nurses what it is like to provide healthcare in the least developed parts of the world. Many had already signed contracts for posts in distant, extremely poor places. I was meant to explain how they should go about their jobs.

That moment, just before the first lecture, was magic. I had never seen such eager and motivated students. They were a little shy of each other, though. Some had chosen this line of work because they were members of the Pentecostal Church, others came from charities with roles in Africa. When we polled the students' voting preferences, the majority of the recruits to the course were either Christian Democrats or left-of-center Social Democrats. Even their dress style provided clues: some had their hair nicely done and wore clean, buttoned-up shirts and blouses, and others slouched in unwashed jeans. But they all showed an intense interest in hearing what I had to say.

"I'm going to introduce this course by telling you an anecdote that I heard from the minister of health in Mozambique," I started, as I pulled the piece of material out from its hiding place. When I was working there as a doctor, I had to struggle with very limited resources. The minister's story was about a very small blanket."

In lectures, timing is all.

"Though the story is really about a man," I went on, pointing at myself. "He was walking in the Mozambican mountains when night fell. He was sleepy but it was cold and all he carried with him was a small blanket. How to make the best use of it?"

At this point, I lay down flat on my back on top of the desk. Some of the students burst out laughing at the weirdness of my behavior. Others looked deadly earnest and a little uncomfortable. All were clearly thrown off balance a little. That was a good thing. I had caught their attention. I scanned the audience.

"I had better wrap the blanket round my feet, the man thought." I put the tiny blanket on my feet. "But then his body became very cold. So instead he put the blanket across his belly." I moved the piece of material to my hips.

"But now both his hands and his feet were freezing. He curled up but it didn't help. He had the idea to wrap the blanket like a turban around his head. That didn't work either. He still couldn't sleep and it made him angry because he was so tired. 'It must be possible to make the blanket bigger,' the man thought."

Now I stood up on the desk, put my foot on one end of the blanket and pulled energetically at the other end.

"I need to make it bigger!" I shouted. And I tore it in half.

The students laughed but were still at a loss to understand what I was really trying to tell them. Immediately, I began to explain.

"Don't react like this man when you work in faraway healthcare systems. Don't push your staff beyond what is reasonable and don't imagine you can offer treatments like those available in Sweden. You must be wise and use 'your blanket' the right way. And don't wear yourselves out. You have to stay in one piece, at least for the duration of the contract. How best to use limited resources in situations of great need is precisely what this course is about."

Goofing around with the blanket was therapeutic for me. I had lived with a great deal of frustration during my years in Mozambique. When I got back to Sweden, I wound up teaching this class from 1983 to 1996. It was the very same course that Agneta and I had attended all those years back, before setting out for Nacala: Healthcare in Underdeveloped Countries. I took on the job because it was easy to combine with my annual field research in Mozambique. Between teaching periods, I could take the research months off with full pay on the condition that I also worked as a consultant to aid organizations. Gradually, my identity changed and I never went back to practicing medicine. I had turned into a scientist and an academic teacher in global healthcare.

The course was divided into three parts. One third was devoted to the care of mothers and children. One third dealt with viral infections in places of extreme poverty. The remaining third concentrated on how to organize and lead a healthcare system that has to function with perhaps as little as 1 percent of the resources available in Sweden. The students were exceptionally motivated: they had all signed on for specific healthcare jobs in some of the most impoverished countries in the world, generally for two years. The first two parts of the course suited them perfectly because the course content was all about how to treat patients.

The third part was more challenging. Everyone easily grasped the importance of learning about malaria and parasitic infections but most were surprised at being asked to learn how to estimate numbers of required staff, or figure out rates for fuel consumption, or draw up an annual budget for a mobile vaccination team. When, at the end of the course, the students were asked to evaluate it, many commented that learning more about laboratory test methods would have been preferable. But after they had been out in the field and were again presented with an evaluation form, the majority said they would have liked to know more about management, staff training, and budgeting. That was why it was such a help in my lectures to draw on the experiences of students who had already worked in low-income countries.

Most of these students had worked for religious missions and learned ineffective methods for recording how their services reached the population, whether it was support for pregnant mothers and maternity care, or the treatment of children with malaria, or injured patients requiring surgery. They had been taught to record how far the patients had traveled to reach the field hospitals or mission clinics, to gauge the effectiveness of the services being offered. When Médecins Sans Frontières (Doctors Without Borders) began their work, it turned out that their staff were also using the same old "How far did the patient travel?" question to determine how well they were serving their populations.

This method takes no account of population demographics.

I taught my students a different, three-stage approach to estimating how healthcare was used by people in the area.

First, get as correct a figure as possible for the number of people who live in the area you serve. Remarkably few of those who had experience of work in distant places had bothered to find this out, despite the facts that all countries conduct a census of some kind and that hospitals usually have defined catchment areas.

Second, get an estimate of how many children are born annually in this catchment area. In poor agricultural regions, the number of children born in a year is approximately 4.5 percent of the population. So, if the region has a population of 100,000, the expected number of newborns is 4,500.

Last, find out what proportion of the children were born with help from healthcare staff. You get this figure by dividing the number of registered births, let's say 1,100 in a year, by the number of expected births (4,500 in this example). The conclusion in this case is that only about a quarter of all births were supported by trained staff and that the other three-quarters of births took place at home with no known skilled assistance.

Looking at vaccinations, if say 2,200 children are vaccinated against measles in one year and you compare that figure with the

Ex cathedra: *perched on the desk*

expected number of new births (4,500 in this example), you soon realize that half the area's children are not getting vaccinated.

These are the important questions. They do not relate to how far patients have had to travel.

Many of my students resisted the notion that they needed such numbers in order to act ethically. They clung to the idea that the ethical choice was to treat those patients who had managed to get to the hospital as effectively as possible. They would not take on board the fact that for the majority of patients in poor countries, to travel was not an option. It was difficult to convince these students that, as the people responsible for healthcare services, they would do more good if they focused on offering the basics, such as iron tablets for pregnant women and vaccines for children, to as many people as possible.

To me, the discussion of how to reach the poorest and most excluded was the core issue in my teaching. It went hand in hand with explaining how significant the differences in health service resources could be between different countries, even though all of them might have been categorized under the one label of "underdeveloped." My explanations drew some strange responses, when students taking the course became aware of how much their target countries had developed over the last few decades. It could even make them disappointed and irritated. One day after lunch, when I returned to my office in the Uppsala Institute for International Child Health, a young woman was waiting for me.

"I wanted to speak to you one-on-one," she said.

The preparatory course, scheduled to run for ten weeks, had only just started but I already recognized her as a very active participant. Her breathing sounded strained as she settled on the visitor's chair next to my desk. Without saying a word, she put a letter in front of me with a hand that trembled a little. I noted the ornate letterhead with its elegant type. The sender was an official in Thailand's Ministry of Health. The long message was written in English.

"This is a rejection of my application for a work permit to be employed as a nurse in Thailand. Can you believe it! They are telling me I can't go there to work in the Baptist-run hospital in northern Thailand. I have been planning it for ages and already signed a contract with the Baptist Mission."

The words poured from her. There was no mistaking how angry and desperate she felt. I was genuinely surprised. Via the Baptist Mission, Sida (the Swedish International Development Cooperation Agency) had funded her pay as a health service volunteer so her services would cost Thailand nothing.

"Exactly! I mean, why refuse?" she said. I did not understand the rationale either. I offered to phone the secretary of the mission, who I knew was very experienced. But, the angry nurse in my office told me, there was no need.

"I have already spoken with him. He explained that it's Thai government policy to encourage hospitals funded by foreign states to employ only Thai nurses. He says there are actually unemployed local Thai nurses, though I find that hard to believe."

I promised her I would look into the matter. She left my office, dejected.

The explanation in the letter from Thailand turned out to be perfectly true. Even back in 1972, Agneta and I had been impressed by the university hospital in Bangkok and, since then, Thailand had gone through a period of rapid social and economic development. In fifteen years the average per capita income had doubled and life expectancy had increased by ten years. It was reasonable that the country would prefer its own nurses to be employed in their home country. For one thing, they of course spoke Thai fluently.

The angry nurse who had been refused a work permit for Thailand was only the first of many students who alerted me to the fact that the world needed different kinds of skills, and so if my course was to continue it would have to start recruiting different kinds of students. That change had already happened by the time I left the Uppsala Institute for International Child Health in 1996, after thirteen years, to take up a post at the Karolinska Institute in Stockholm. By then, the students in my course were mostly qualified doctors and nurses who had short-term contracts to work for Médecins Sans Frontières at emergency clinics in disaster zones. Many so-called "underdeveloped countries" had followed the same route as Thailand and even countries that were still very poor, like Tanzania and Mozambique, had as many local doctors and nurses as they could afford to employ. Indeed, Africa had already begun to "export" healthcare staff to Western Europe and the Middle East. The old kind of Western doctor who had worked in African missions for ten or twenty years was no longer needed and no longer existed, and similarly there was no longer any need for Western doctors and nurses serving for a few years in aid organizations.

I had been very engaged in teaching throughout these years but I did not hesitate when offered a chance to return to research work—by a man from the Cuban embassy who turned up in my office one day in 1993.

He brought me a bottle of rum, arguably not the most appropriate gift to bring an expert in public health, and had an urgent reason for calling: an epidemic had started spreading in Cuba over the last few months. Characteristically, Castro's regime had advised the media to keep quiet. The first sign of illness was a loss of sensation in the toes and then in both legs. The weakness could become so pronounced that the patient could barely walk. Sometimes, the sensory loss also included their fingers. As the condition progressed, the patient's sight deteriorated, with large blind spots in their field of vision and changes in color perception. The underlying nerve damage was clearly very serious; worse still, the number of cases was truly alarming, at more than forty thousand.

"We have decided to ask foreign scientists to study this condition and we would love you to look into it," the embassy official said.

I was certainly curious: scientifically speaking, the symptomatology was really exciting. But how should I design the research investigation?

It did not take me long to realize that the embassy official wasn't here to inquire about my interest; he was a messenger from someone who had already decided that he wanted my help. I was known for having investigated poisoning caused by cassava— roots that were also eaten in Cuba.

"Can you come next week?" the embassy official asked me.

"What are you suggesting? Why didn't you come to see me earlier and give me more warning?" I asked.

My daughter's end-of-school exams were scheduled for the following week. In Sweden, this event, with all the surrounding ceremony, is a key rite of passage. I asked him if I could stay until after the ceremony, and then leave immediately afterward. He agreed.

"Good. But the research will cost a lot. Do you have the money to fund it?"

"Regrettably, we don't," he said. "Because of the crisis."

At the time, Cuba was in the grip of a financial crisis that they had named *el período especial*, "the special period." The Soviet Union, Cuba's major trading partner, had initially saved the island economy, but the Soviet Union itself was going through its own political convulsions and collapse. Now, most everyday goods in Cuba, including food, were rationed, bus services were canceled, and electricity came on for a couple of hours in the evening but only in alternating districts. This was how the regime was trying to solve its problems, which, according to their frequently reiterated argument, were caused by *el bloqueo*—the blockade by the

USA. In Cuba, they also spoke, but only in whispers, of *el bloqueo interno*—the internal blockade. For instance, you could not buy bananas in the streets of Havana because the farmers who grew them had to sell their produce to the state-owned company. This was due not to US sanctions but to the rigidity of state planning.

I applied to Sida for travel funds and was offered a grant within forty-eight hours. The team at Sida were not fans of the Cuban government, but the Cuban population was obviously suffering.

Preparations were made swiftly. Before long I was on a flight to Havana with Per Lundquist, a chemist from Linköping University. Once we arrived, we were in Cuban hands. "We'll meet you at the airport," they had told us. As soon as we descended the steps from the plane we were led away and driven to a VIP lounge where we were welcomed by a large reception committee. Two obviously important figures singled themselves out from the crowd: a man with crisply pressed trousers and polished shoes, and a woman wearing very red lipstick. The man introduced himself as the deputy minister of health and the woman as director of the Finlay Research Institute. Its name commemorated the Cuban epidemiologist Carlos Finlay, who had discovered that yellow fever is spread by mosquitoes.

I was discreetly informed that the woman, known as Conchita, was also a member of the politburo. It was clear that this was a very big thing: a member of the highest echelons of the Cuban Communist Party had come to meet me.

The following day we were collected from the hotel and driven to the Finlay Institute. The Cuban medical scientists who had been working on the epidemic—epidemiologists, clinicians, and laboratory scientists—were waiting to meet us. The atmosphere was tense with expectation. I felt like water in the desert, so eager were the Cubans to talk to foreign colleagues. Their presentations about the epidemic, who had been afflicted and where, were first class. Most of the cases had been found in Pinar del Río, a tobacco-growing province. We all lunched together and then returned to the laboratories, but we had hardly started working before the main door suddenly opened and several men came in. They moved about without making a sound because they all wore gym shoes. Each carried a handgun in his holster. They positioned themselves in the corners of the lab.

Then the boss entered. Fidel Castro.

I caught sight of his profile and just had time to think, "That's Fidel Castro." I had seen him on TV before and heard excerpts of his shouty speeches. The man now in front of me reminded me of the generously bearded Beppe Wolgers, the Swedish actor and poet. Castro gave himself time to greet the people in the room and ask after everyone's families. When he caught sight of me, he broke into a slow jog and advanced toward me with open arms: *"El sueco!"* he exclaimed—the Swede!

I introduced my Swedish colleague but Castro was obviously more interested in me.

"What were you discussing when I came in?" he asked.

I told him about the course I was teaching and Castro asked questions about Mozambique and its socialist president.

"So, you worked in Mozambique when Samora Machel was president, and as a young man you joined the Social Democrats?"

At first, I couldn't think where he was going with this. Then I realized that he had memorized my CV and was checking it.

"May I say something?" I decided to ask.

"Yes," he replied, sounding a little curious.

"Mr. President, I would like to thank you personally, on behalf of all public health researchers. You have stated publicly that you have stopped smoking, even though you have long been identified with a fondness for large cigars. Indeed, you are in charge of a tobacco-producing country. It was a very significant statement."

He laughed. The others in the room laughed with him, in a manner that is characteristic of people who work under a dictator. It is artificial laughter but not false; well-meaning but going on for a little too long. The dictators appreciate it for what it is: a show of respect.

Once Castro had left the room, our discussions resumed. The Cubans were intensely serious about their task and were happy to have us, but they must have wondered exactly why we were there—the epidemic was actually on the wane. However, they still did not know what had caused it. The intention behind our invitation was probably two-fold. In the first place, it was important to establish that the epidemic was not infectious. Second our presence showed the Cuban people that the country was open to international science.

The following day we were shown around hospitals in the capital and introduced to patients. In the ophthalmology department, I was impressed by the advanced treatments available for patients with sight problems. Consultants and groups of doctors specialized in discrete conditions such as cataract surgery, glaucoma, diabetic retinopathy, and so on. My Cuban colleagues responded to my curiosity and relished my clear admiration.

That evening a meeting had been arranged for us with members of the politburo and the Academy of Sciences. We met in one of the academy's meeting rooms in its official home, a three-story concrete block. I had been asked to tell them about my impressions of the Finlay Institute and the hospitals we had been taken to see.

The conversation began smoothly but then I moved on to question their methods. Finding out what individuals have been eating is one of the most difficult things to investigate, even when the subject does their best to describe everything in detail. The inquiry must establish not only *what* the subject has eaten but also how much of each item, how it was cooked, and where it came from.

"I think you have been using the wrong methodology to find out about people's food intake," I said. "You have simply handed them a questionnaire. How can you be sure that what is written down is a correct account? For one thing, what about any informal trade in food stuffs? Is it possible that some toxic component might have been smuggled into Cuba?"

"The island is shut off so that's impossible!" someone exclaimed.

They laughed but were clearly feeling defensive—not because they were loyal Cubans but because they were very skilled quantitative epidemiologists. They had mastered and refined numerical methods for calculating and comparing exposure to risk factors between groups of ill and well people. It was a bit much to ask them to tolerate an anthropological approach that called for varying questions asked in an open interview format, and which even assessed facial expressions and body language. To them this was fluffy methodology. At the time, in the 1990s, there was strong opposition between these two different ways of working.

Suddenly, the door opened and the silent men in gym shoes entered and distributed themselves into the corners of the room once again.

Castro followed. As before, I had had no pre-warning. Later, I realized that the entire meeting in the Academy of Sciences had actually been engineered to create a meeting between me and Fidel Castro.

He sat down in the armchair next to me. I praised the presentations we had seen.

"What do we do now?" he asked.

"My job is to find out whether something people have eaten might have caused the epidemic."

"But the team have already investigated everything."

"No, they have not investigated everything, because they relied on questionnaires. The list of questions focused only on the topics the investigators had already considered. No one has investigated what hasn't yet been considered."

The methodology discussion started all over again.

"Are people really telling the truth about what they have eaten? After all, the epidemic occurred during a *período especial*," I said.

He interrupted me and his tone was now harsher.

"I assure you, the Cuban people have the greatest confidence in our health service."

We were at a conversational dead end and no longer understood each other. Castro was visibly irritated and the Cuban scientists and officials shifted about restlessly in the large room, looking as expressionless as fish, while some exchanged pained glances, then stared down at the table top. They seemed eager to leave the room.

"May I tell you a story?" I asked.

I heard the words coming from my mouth. Castro seemed a little uneasy.

"A story? Of course, go ahead." Our eyes met.

"When I was a young student, I watched footage of you and Che Guevara arriving here in Havana. You had come from Mexico in the ship *Granma* to start the Cuban revolution."

"You have seen it?"

"Yes. It was filmed in black-and-white."

"Do you remember the moment we stepped on land?"

"No, I don't. I remember seeing you on board the ship. And then you were on land."

"True. We never filmed the landing."

A typical dictator's device, testing me.

"But I saw the footage of the time when you lived among the people in the Sierra Maestra. You learned about their living conditions. You had been a privileged student beforehand and had never lived among people in remote regions. At first, you did not understand them."

"That's true," he said.

"I remember seeing you sleeping in a small wooden shack and working with the Sierra people in the fields. You helped the children with their homework and the women with the cooking. You must have come to understand them well?"

"Yes. I understood them," he said.

"Still there was one thing that surprised me. Something I did *not* see in the film. It was completely absent."

"What do you mean?"

"There were no questionnaires!"

Most of the listeners could not see the point but Castro did and he laughed.

"I want to follow your example and do what you did. I want to take a team of researchers to Pinar del Río and find out exactly how people live. We might find something unexpected. This kind of research is what I call open-ended," I explained.

Then I added a sentence that made Castro's face really light up.

"Today, your approach in the Sierra Maestra has become research methodology."

He left after that. No agreement had been reached.

The following morning, two men were waiting for me when I came down for breakfast. One of them wore a military uniform and stood to attention. The other was a civilian. They were, respectively, the Cuban commander in chief and the minister of health. Their message was that *El Comandante* wanted me to stay for six months, with complete freedom to plan my work.

My head spun. Six months? There I sat, facing two of Cuba's most senior state officials, who insisted that I should stay. At home in Sweden, my family was waiting for me. I had intended to spend the summer with them. I must phone Agneta.

"Oh, it's you!" Agneta said at the other end of the line.

We had not been in touch since my arrival in Cuba, so I began by describing the situation in general. Later, I would have to be specific.

"Gosh! Have you really met Castro?" she exclaimed.

I told her what the Cuban government had in mind and suggested that I should stay for three months. Halfway through my time here, she and the children could come to Cuba for a week's holiday.

Agneta stayed quiet and listened carefully.

"Sounds good," she said, in her usual straightforward way.

The following day, we had to plan. We began by drawing up detailed maps of the geographical spread of the epidemic. I had been allocated a few additional Cuban colleagues to help with the work, including Mariluz Rodriguez, the epidemiologist in charge of the most affected province. She had worked in Angola for a long time and was incredibly good at her job. Mariluz was frank and spontaneous. Professionally, we had a lot in common. She had a mane of red, curly hair and wore very red lipstick. It was clearly a national style choice. I had never seen such bright lipstick as in Cuba.

It was thanks to Mariluz that I came to understand what the Cuban crisis, that special period, really meant. One Saturday night, she had invited me round to have a meal with her and her husband. He was sitting next to her, holding her hands because they were so sore. It had been laundry day: the family's clothes and bedlinen had to be washed by hand in a cement trough with a corrugated inner side. Since neither washing powder, liquid soap, nor ordinary soap was available to buy, Mariluz used salt, which ruined the skin on her hands. It was remarkable: one of the leading specialists employed to control an ongoing epidemic had had to spend half her Saturday laundering sheets in salt solution. Still, Mariluz supported the regime. She called herself a revolutionary and was proud of the achievements of the revolution, especially the health service. She had been there from the beginning and had devoted her life to working in public health, including the eventual control of tuberculosis and the introduction of decent toilets for everyone. Being part of the Cuban health service was a source of great pride.

We began our investigation by conducting what I call semi-quantitative interviews with two different groups: one group was from an area with many patients who suffered from paralysis and the other was from one with few. From the data, it emerged that in areas where there were private farms they had very few or no cases. After the revolution, Cuba's large farms had been nationalized but the smaller ones had been left in private hands.

In order to interview the farmers in peace, away from the prying eyes and ears of the regime, we employed a method that I had devised in Africa. When we first arrived in a community, I would spend time with the local power brokers. In the party meeting rooms, decorated with pictures of Lenin and Marx, I held court with the secret police, who were curious about the foreign doctor. To make myself look important, I brought along a list of questions for them, all unrelated to the investigation. I also offered to measure everyone's blood pressure. Meanwhile, the interviewers—junior doctors who were all women—were given the space and time to chat with the local village women and carry out the job they had come to do. Much can be managed by manipulating people's curiosity.

While I was working in Cuba, Castro would often mention me and my work and the state newspaper would write up stories about "the Swedish doctor" who had sacrificed his family holiday to come and work in Cuba. Castro told his people that "you won't get any holiday either" and many citizens became angry with me.

The party bosses wanted me to appear on state TV to explain my research. I managed to get out of that. Working in a dictatorship requires you to be very precise about your role. Why was I working in Cuba? My task was to try to understand the cause of the epidemic. While I was there, I must not quarrel with the authorities but also must avoid being exploited by them. Above all, I must not be a source of harm to my colleagues. It is essential for the visitor to accept that local people live with certain constraints. For example, the kinds of conversations that Swedes might take for granted were kept strictly private and simply never took place in public in Cuba. You must be alert to the signals that someone is prepared to speak openly, but you cannot force their decision.

My family did come to spend a holiday with me and then my daughter, Anna, stayed for a while longer. She had made friends of her own age in Cuba and went dancing with them in salsa bars. Her friends had cars, but to use them they needed petrol bought on the black market. My daughter visited apartments where black-market fuel was stored in bathtubs and she haggled over prices with drivers. She got a lot of insight into the trade in goods, including the prices; we had developed a new investigative methodology known as daughter-goes-dancing-and-talks-to-the-locals. When she came back after a night on the town, I would sit on her bedside asking for details until she pleaded that she was exhausted and just wanted to go to sleep.

Anna's stories about the nightlife in Pinar del Río really helped me to understand more about Cuban society and the role of the black market. At breakfast, while Anna still slept, I would tell my fellow epidemiologists about our latest findings.

During the daytime we collected data and, in the evenings, we would collate and tabulate what we had learned. By midnight we had usually finished work and the guitars came out. There was always someone who played "*Cuba, qué linda es Cuba,*" "Cuba, how lovely is Cuba." I fixed beers for everyone from our foreigners' rations—my allowance was two or three bottles per day.

As time went by, we found we could now draw a graph based on our data, a curve showing the number of new cases per day. And were there any aspects of the graph that coincided with external events? We could observe social factors: those who had contacts in foreign countries were less affected, for example. There were about ten thousand cases of the illness in Pinar del Río. As we initially noted, small-scale farmers were much less afflicted than the workers in large tobacco plantations, who tended to be undernourished.

It seemed unrealistic to imagine that the Cuban government was unaware of the black market. Nonetheless, my colleagues had never heard of any state registration of the black market pricing systems.

"Quite out of the question," they assured me.

I did not believe them.

"Come on, can't we speak with the provincial governor? He should know, shouldn't he?"

Everything about this idea made my colleagues feel uneasy, but they agreed to book me an appointment with him. The governor was seated at a desk overflowing with papers when he received our delegation. I outlined our findings so far, stressing that farmers who worked on small, privately owned farms escaped the illness, while plantation workers who had relatively little to eat were often afflicted.

The governor was very interested and enthusiastic.

"We believe that people who can afford to buy food from unofficial sources are protected against the illness. Are you aware of how the prices move in the market?"

Now he became serious.

"What do you mean?" he asked.

"Well, let me explain. In Sweden there is no shortage of food. However, we do struggle with the trade in illegal drugs—a problem you don't seem to have here."

I launched into a vivid account of how drug-dependent Sweden had become.

"Heroin, amphetamines, cannabis. All on the black market, of course. Still, the police do what they can, using informers who report back on prices in the market. They can determine when a delivery has come in because the prices fall."

"Now that's very interesting! We use the same approach here," He looked at us all in turn. "We call it *Instituto de la Demanda Interna*—that is, the Institute for Internal Demand."

My colleagues had gone silent and the atmosphere was tense.

"Would it be possible for us to see someone at the institute?" I asked cautiously.

Castro had given me the all-clear, after all. Before long, we were standing outside a modest, unmarked door.

"We have been expecting you," said the man who opened the door.

Inside, a large woman sat waiting for us. Her shape was startling—food was scarce that summer and it was rare to see anyone overweight in Cuba. She told us that her unit was in charge of compiling data on oil and meat prices. In a dark room with drawn curtains we were shown the data and allowed to copy down the figures by hand.

While the head of the unit and I got into a discussion about the best method of collecting data, as one would with a professional colleague, my companions kept quiet.

They remained silent in the taxi back to the hotel, but once we sat down together to talk, I said enthusiastically:

"See, I told you they had something like this!"

I was thrilled with my findings and felt a little superior. But then I sensed the atmosphere: the others were subdued, even sad.

"Unbelievable! This is completely unbelievable. How is it possible that *you* should discover this? You, a foreigner who has been here for a month! I trusted that our state would not be run in this way. Clearly, I'm more revolutionary than the revolutionaries," one of them burst out, looking at a colleague.

A wise regime that finds itself unable to feed its population will allow the black market to manage its trading but under supervision. Cubans had fought for a new society and believed they could live without free enterprise, but found they needed it to survive. The bright red lipstick, for example, was imported by sports teams, who went shopping when they competed abroad. Lipsticks were perfect for the black market: they combined high value with low volume and were easy to transport. Of course, not everyone could afford one, but there would be a lipstick owner in most tenement staircases. You sought her out when you needed a boost and paid her a fee in return for a slick of color on your lips.

Our investigation into Cuba's paralyzing illness came to a close when we demonstrated that the epidemic was unquestionably linked to people's monotonous diet, triggered by the food shortage after the fall of the Soviet Union. Many would fall ill because they gave any meat and eggs available to the children and the elderly. The most heroic Cubans survived on rice and sugar, an extremely dangerous diet, lacking in vitamins or protein. Sugar was always available on the black market—the Cubans joked about it: breakfast was *sopa de gallina*—meaning chicken soup, but actually now redefined as just sugary water.

The results of our investigation were handed over to the government and my Swedish colleague and I returned home. Before we left, we promised not to describe the condition in our official report as "toxic nutritional," that is, as a combination of undernourishment and poisoning. It was too politically sensitive to say the food supply in Cuba was insufficient. Instead, the favored classification was "toxic metabolic," indicating that non-poisonous substances had been metabolized into toxins in the body.

We had had no warning about the gathering at Stockholm airport, where a team from Swedish state television was waiting to interview us on our arrival. I was quite unprepared and had not discussed with the Cuban authorities how I was to handle publicity in Sweden. I ought to have told Castro before I left that, in my country, ignoring questions from the media was not an option.

The news agency Reuters cabled the news of our findings worldwide: Eminent Swedish doctor says food in Cuba was so scarce and bad it made people ill. The Cuban government did not take kindly to my statement and our collaboration ceased. I didn't talk about the investigation again.

But time passed and things calmed down. Several years later, I was invited back to Cuba to give a lecture to the Ministry of Health on "Cuban Health from a Global Perspective." In my lecture, I pointed out that Cuba's child mortality rates were the same as those in the United States, despite its comparatively much lower per capita income. I was wildly applauded. After my presentation, the minister leaped up on stage and thanked me very warmly.

"We Cubans are the healthiest of the poor!" he exclaimed.

Later, a young man joined me at the coffee machine. He took my arm and gently led me away from the crowd. Then he leaned toward me and whispered:

"Your data is correct, but the minister's conclusion is wrong. We are not the healthiest of the poor—we are the poorest of the healthy."

Then he walked away. He left me with a smile on my face because he was right. What was remarkable about Cuba was not their advanced health service but the colossal failure of the regime to create economic growth and freedom of expression.

To this day, I have never published the results of my investigations in Cuba. I did not want to create problems for the people I had been working with there. Nowhere in the world had I come to care more for my colleagues.*

The task I was given in Cuba was unusually dramatic and very unlike most research, which is often dull. Persistence is the most important characteristic of a researcher. But now and then there are moments, often years apart, when you have the hugely gratifying feeling of having discovered something.

By 1996, I was running a five-week course in global health at the Karolinksa Institute in Stockholm. It was a very popular course,

---

* Hans Rosling's Cuban research was published after his death by the family in collaboration with his Cuban co-writers. It appeared in 2017 in a special edition of the Swedish *Socialmedicinsk tidskrift* (Social Medical Journal) about Hans Rosling. See "Ecological studies in Pinar del Rio Province support a toxico-nutritional etiology of epidemic neuropathy in Cuba" in *Socialmedicinsk tidskrift*, vol. 94, no. 6, 2017, pp. 731–745.

not least because the students spent the last two weeks abroad. Every term, our course would be chosen by around thirty of the institute's one hundred medical students.

But after a couple of years a new idea took root in my mind: I was concerned that the course was only attracting those students who already knew about global health. I wanted instead for the course to be compulsory for all medical students. To present this plan convincingly, I needed evidence that, before they joined the course, our students knew much more about the topic than others. One of my graduate students, Robin Brittain-Long, offered to have a go at finding out if this was true. We agreed that Robin would compare two groups, one of students who had chosen my course and one of students who had chosen a course in intensive care, a subject with wider appeal.

When Robin first showed me the results of the study, I was rather disappointed. It showed that prospective students with an interest in global health knew no more about the subject than those who had decided to take the intensive care course. Shit, that's me proved wrong, I thought.

But then I looked more closely at Robin's data and what I saw made the hair on my arms stand on end and a shiver run down my spine. My heart beat faster and I almost stopped breathing when I realized just how awful the results were. One question was especially revealing: "Below are five pairs of countries. In each pair, one country has a child mortality rate twice as high, or more, than the other. Please select the country with the higher mortality rate." All the pairs consisted of one European and one non-European country. Child mortality is one of the most useful measures of a country's socioeconomic development. To choose the correct answer in each pair, the student needed a rough idea of which country was the more developed. Given that there were only two options, if they picked countries at random, half of the answers should have been right.

Yet the students managed to get only 36 percent right, which means they performed worse than if they had known nothing and relied on luck.

This was why the hair on my arms stood on end: responses that were worse than chance implied some incorrect assumption or prejudice. Far too many of the students assumed that child mortality would always be lower in Europe than in some rapidly growing Asian countries. However, by 1999, South Korea had less than half the child mortality of Poland, which was also true of Sri Lanka compared to Turkey, and Malaysia compared to Russia.

When I had calmed down, I realized that Robin's study opened up a startling new perspective: education about global health was not about filling knowledge gaps. Its proper function was to remove preconceived opinions, particularly that "the West" is always more developed than anywhere else in the world. The other key finding was that even students with a strong interest in the world around them did not necessarily know more about it than their less-interested peers.

A quarter of a century had passed since Agneta and I had been shocked at our own unpreparedness for the advances we saw in Southeast Asia. Twenty-five years later these Swedish students still had not noticed how quickly that part of the world had been catching up with Europe, and that many Asian countries were now doing better in some respects than parts of Europe.

Before taking up the post at the Karolinska Institute, I had spent almost ten years teaching global trends in healthcare and population growth at the University of Uppsala. I had met many smart, highly motivated students with strongly held, preconceived ideas about what was going on in the rest of the world. It was obvious that the Swedish education system had failed to give them even a rudimentary knowledge about the world beyond Europe.

I told them that, globally, healthcare was improving steadily but they would argue back. My data must be wrong, they said,

since they knew for a fact that environmental decay was causing more and more damage to public health. I also told them
that the rate of population growth had been decreasing for the
last twenty-five years and they countered by saying that no, the
world's population was growing faster than ever. Furthermore,
they had learned that population growth was the major cause of
environmental destruction. Some of them cared more for dead
animals than the millions of dead children in poor countries. I
tried to explain that the gorillas would have no future unless there
were dramatic improvements in the living conditions of the people
with whom they shared their habitat.

Time and time again, year after year, the same things were said
in the same tone of voice. There were usually small groups of
fanatical, emotional individuals and others who seemed calmer
and more matter-of-fact. Each year, the majority of students
tended to side with the activists.

This was during the 1990s, when a lot of public interest was
focused on animal conservation rather than climate change. The
extinction "red lists" were public and it was clear that many animals were at risk. Yet even organizations like the World Wide
Fund for Nature grasped that saving the chimpanzees was impossible unless the people in the region had a decent standard of
living. The activists, though, were not prepared to follow that line
of thought.

For a few years, I would go home thinking about the students'
ideology and condemning it. Their most deeply rooted notion was
that there were two different types of people, who lived in two
different types of countries. When I sat in the cafes and listened to
their conversations, I heard the world discussed in terms of "us" and
"them". The most common statements were endlessly repeated:
"They simply can't expect to live the way we do now, it wouldn't
work. Imagine if all Chinese people owned a car!"

In my view the students were right to say that it was going
to be impossible for everyone to end up consuming resources at

the current rate of the world's wealthiest nations. But it was the wealthy nations who were going to have to reduce their consumption. The poorest should consume more while the large middle group should follow the wealthiest toward sustainable levels of consumption. Few students agreed with me, because the majority seemed convinced that the poor led contented lives in rain forests and small rural villages. Their insistence shocked me deeply. I remembered only too well how much people in poor parts of the world desired electricity, running water, roads, and access to education and healthcare.

Every academic year we created new courses and I took on the challenge of teaching a new batch of students about life at different levels of economic development. Above all, I tried to explain that there is no valid distinction between "us" and "them". People are much the same all over the world, with standards of living that can be mapped on a continuous scale.

I would start my course by handing out oversize sheets of paper showing tables 1 to 5 from UNICEF's annual report on children worldwide. The data sets for each country covered population size, economic development and health status, and included current data as well as the figures for the past year and twenty years ago. I asked the students to examine the tables and pick out the most successful countries. Clearly, if you looked at birth rates and child survival rates, the world could no longer be divided into two groups.

Most of the students proved resistant to facts. They claimed that the data from developing countries must be wrong. During the breaks and the Q&A sessions they explained to me that the population explosion was due to an increased birth rate among Africans, Muslims, and poor people—and that the rate at which these children died was the one thing that kept populations under control. I referred them to the data in front of them, which had come from the most reliable source within the United Nations, and said:

"Many decades have passed since child mortality acted as a

check on population growth. The fastest population growth is now found in the poorest countries with the highest child mortality: people living in extreme poverty have more children because they need child labor and because they know some of their children might die. The only way forward is to carry on working to reduce both poverty and child deaths. Once parents see that children survive, they will want fewer, better-educated children. That is when you need to prioritize access to contraception."

I was then, and still am, baffled at how hard this is to explain.

Several students would always reply that if these children lived, animals would die. I would go over it again: if more children lived, mothers would choose to have fewer children and the population size would stabilize, which would be in the interest of the animals as well. The main global health priority had to be to reduce child mortality in the poorest countries. One afternoon, a student stood up at the back of the theater and shouted at the top of his voice: "You're like Hitler toward the animals!"

When I returned home at ten o'clock that evening, I realized it was time to accept that the way I was presenting the facts was not working. How could I demonstrate that their binary system did not exist? How could I show them that the world corresponded neither to the colonial concept of East and West, nor to the newer subdivision of North and South?

Then an idea came to me: I would represent each country as a bubble and its size would be proportional to the population size. If I drew a graph on which the horizontal axis showed income per head and the vertical axis provided an indicator of national health, like life expectancy or the number of surviving children per family, I could place the population bubbles onto it. That evening, I spent several hours on the first prototype. I used datasets from UNICEF's yearbook and entered them into the statistics program StatView. By bedtime, I had printed out my prototype and put a copy in my rucksack. I wanted to test it out on my students as soon as possible.

The results were promising. The students seemed to like the idea of this new kind of world map. At that point, I could not foresee how significantly these bubbles would change my life.

The crucial step was taken one winter day in Stockholm in 1996. I hurried through the slushy snow, clutching a bundle of documents, on my way to the Karolinska Institute, where I was to be interviewed for the position of Chair in International Health. Being short-listed was more than I had expected, because several of the other applicants were much better qualified than me. So I had a plan for how to make a good impression.

When I arrived, the chairman of the committee, Professor Erling Norrby, asked me to step inside and sit at one end of an oval table. Eight professors, all older than me, were seated around the table. The sharp light of the winter day flooded in through a large widow and made their faces indistinct. Professor Norrby addressed me:

"Hans Rosling, you are our last candidate. We would like you to explain to us what you consider to be the core issues in the field of international health. And then please tell us why you are the right person to be appointed."

I replied that the key fields of study were global variations in health and healthcare provision, and how best to promote and restore health among the poorest people. Then I continued:

"However, I don't plan to convince you why I should be appointed. I'm aware that several of the other applicants are much better qualified than me. Instead, I am going to put you in the best possible position to choose the right person for the post by using my twenty minutes to teach you some fundamental things about global variations in health. I have studied the lists of your publications and know that none of you is an expert in this area. So, I have prepared copies of a colored bubble graph for you. Every bubble is a country and the color denotes its continent. The vertical axis shows life expectancy and the horizontal shows per capita income."

I pointed to some examples: "Look, the range of countries runs from the Congo in the bottom left, where lives are short and the population is very poor, up to Japan in the top right, where lives are long and average income is high."

I went on to explain the irrelevance of a binary division of the world into developed and underdeveloped countries, pointing out that most countries were clustered in the middle of the chart. I also argued that the disease burden gradually changed as economic development progressed, shifting from infections with or without malnutrition to non-infectious diseases, or predominantly late-onset, chronic conditions.

I kept the tempo up so that none of my interviewers would have time to be annoyed at the implication that they were incompetent. I actually found it good fun. My talk held their attention and even got a few positive comments. At the end, they asked me a few more questions and thanked me for my contribution. That same evening I learned that my friend Staffan Bergström had been appointed to the chair, as expected.

The true surprise, though, came the following morning when the telephone rang.

"Good morning, Hans. This is Erling, chairman of the international health appointment committee. You did not get the post, but we were so impressed by your presentation that we would like to offer you a six-year contract as Senior Lecturer."

I took the post. A few years later, I was appointed to a professorship at the Karolinska Institute. My research had taken me as far as the interview short list but my teaching idea, with its use of colorful bubbles, had made me a professor.

6

From the Lecture Theater to Davos

The decisive reactions to my bubble graph were neither those of the Karolinska Institute professors nor those of my students. The responses which had by far the biggest influence on my future professional life came from my son, Ola, and perhaps even more so, from his wife, Anna.

Ola and Anna, both twenty-three years old, had come for supper one evening in September 1998. They lived in Gothenburg at the time but were visiting Uppsala for the weekend. Anna had completed a course in cultural sociology and was now studying at the School of Photography at the university. Ola was studying economic history but his plan was simply to accumulate enough university exam passes to qualify for grants. He wanted to use the money to buy paint and, with his new portfolio, apply for a place at the College of Art, where he had already been short-listed for two years running.

We were about to start on the dessert when I showed them my new, excitingly colorful bubble graph. Instantly, I caught their attention. They were even more curious when I outlined the fact-resistant attitudes of my students who refused to accept that the countries of the world were scattered along a continuous line, from poverty to wealth. Anna asked for a copy to take back to Gothenburg. She displayed it on the wall in their apartment, where their friends would easily see it. At the time, I had no notion that this would be the start of a lifelong collaboration with Anna and Ola, marrying together my obsession with numbers and their artistic talents. You never know where supper with the family might take you.

A couple of weeks later, on September 16, 1998, I received an email from Ola with the subject line: "Ola tries something new." Ola recounted enthusiastically how he had joined an instructive session in a magazine production workshop, run by the Gothenburg Cultural Center, and had heard about a new computer animation program. He ended the email with: "And this is the good news. In the next two months, I plan to use the animation program Director 6.0 and make your graph of Child Mortality v. GNP come alive. If you'd like me to, that is? Please let me know." My boring reply was: "Sounds great, go ahead." I had not the slightest clue what Ola was on about.

A few more weeks had passed when Ola phoned to tell me that he could make the bubbles move but to work on it he needed a more powerful home computer. He wanted to follow up his idea of tweaking the digital version of the graph to make the country bubbles move from one year to the next. The user could then see how and where the world was changing with time. He asked me nicely if I would lend him the money for a new computer. His computer had been a gift from me twelve years ago.

So, what did I say? Just a few years later I would be lauded for showing off the very program that Ola and Anna went on to build for me. At the time, I suspected that Ola wanted the computer to make an animated cartoon to add to his art portfolio. He had already studied at a few different colleges, taken a handful of courses and then worked with a theater in Stockholm. "He had better get used to being short of money if he plans to make a living as an artist," I said to myself, my mind clouded by dull parental thoughts. "No, Ola. I've already given you my old computer," I told him. "Surely that will do." Ola tried to explain that creating moving images required something more sophisticated but I didn't really listen.

The following day, Ola phoned again to tell me that a bank had agreed to lend him the money but they wanted the signature of a guarantor. I still did not listen properly and blocked off his enthusiasm and persistence. Once more, my reply was "No."

It still pains me to confess my behavior. The sum he wanted wouldn't have been a big drain on the family coffers. I was showing a complete inability to *hear* what Ola was really saying. Still, he did not give up and bought a computer on credit, from a friend. Then he managed to get himself a key to the Cultural Center's magazine workshop, where he taught himself programming at night during the autumn of 1998. There he wrote the code for the first animated graph of what he called the "Historical World Health Chart." Anna designed the links. They showed it to me when they were staying with us that Christmas. I remember catching my breath and my eyes widening as the bubbles slowly, smoothly moved from illness and poverty in the lower left-hand corner of the graph, and up toward wealth and longevity in the upper right-hand corner.

"And, look at this—you can track a country! I'll do Sweden for you," Ola said, and smiled. The bubbles moved from 1820 to 1997 again for all the countries, but this time Sweden left a trail of bubble markers, one every five years. It was a small innovation but it enabled us to follow the course of Sweden's path through the last two centuries and compare it with the development of other countries. As the cursor stopped on a bubble, you saw the name of the country and, when the cursor followed the Swedish trail, it showed the year Sweden had reached this or that level of public health or average income.

Wow!

"We must apply for money to develop this idea even further!" I exclaimed spontaneously.

But it turned out to be extremely difficult to get any funding from the sources that would usually give me research grants. As the funding delay continued, Agneta decided to lend Anna and Ola enough for a computer each so that they could work from home, and I began to use the animated bubble graph in my lectures.

Previously, I had been invited to speak only as far afield as Copenhagen. My new tool kit changed this. Out of the blue, I heard from Geneva. The head of statistics at the WHO wanted me to give a talk and later commented: "I've never seen anything like it."

Then Sida—Sweden's state aid organization—decided to support our peculiar project. Anna and Ola gave up their studies and employed skilled coders to work on new visualizations of the data set. *Dollar Street*, Anna's idea, was one of these programs.

These applications elevated my lectures to new levels and made it much easier for me to complete what I saw as my vocation: raising awareness among university students and aid workers as to what was really happening in global development. That was why I held out against a request from the Ministry of Foreign Affairs to appear on the so-called International Square at that year's book fair in Gothenburg.

Why would I hire myself out to chat about world development to the public at large? I had only ever given talks to academic audiences. Besides, I was skeptical about private enterprise: even the book fair seemed too commercial for my liking. The foreign affairs people had to nag me to attend, but finally I caved in and went to Gothenburg.

The hall housing the International Square was large enough for all conceivable aid organizations and international charities to set out their stalls. In front of the speakers' stage, twenty chairs had been arranged for the audience, yet people moving around on the "square" were unable to see the screen on which I projected my imagery. I disapproved of this and twisted the screen to face outward. It meant that my audience had to stand to see but, because the screen could now be seen from the walkway connecting the hall to the rest of the fair, my audience was now almost a hundred rather than just twenty people.

On that day in September 2003, a man called Bo Ekman stopped to listen to my talk. When I had finished speaking, people queued to talk to me and Ekman waited his turn.

"Heads of industry should hear you speak," he said. "What I heard was awfully good."

He surprised me. Bo Ekman, a conventional-looking man in an unremarkable suit, was a major name in Swedish industry. He certainly did not fit easily into the group of a hundred-odd people who had listened to me. He looked ordinary but everything he said was interesting.

Bo asked me to come and speak at the next AGM of Tällberg, a foundation he had started twenty years earlier. The annual meeting was a kind of forum where politicians, academics, and industrialists met and discussed the great issues of the future. I was curious and accepted his invitation.

I suddenly had a completely new audience, including the bosses of Sweden's biggest industries, men and women I had only read about in the newspapers. After my account of the world, they approached me with very insightful questions. That meeting at Tällberg was the start of a fascinating journey.

I was surprised and dismayed to find that the executives of the very largest companies were very well-informed about how the world was changing, much more so than my committed, internationally minded students and aid-organization staff. These business executives needed a grip on facts or their firms would collapse. They had to keep track.

Many public-health experts are deeply suspicious of private enterprise, believing it is all about flogging tobacco and alcohol products or fast cars. After giving so many lectures to staff in private-sector organizations, I acquired a respect for commerce that I had previously lacked because of my working-class background.

We received more and more invitations to demonstrate our

new, fact-based representations of the world. We were asked to speak at conferences all over the world and also had a terrific number of requests for computer-based images of other statistical data sets. Almost all the organizations contacting us had built large databases only to find it hard to convey the meaning of their data—they ranged from UNESCO, the World Bank, and UNICEF to the Swedish local authorities and Rio de Janeiro's town planners.

If we had been capitalists at heart, we would surely have jumped at the chance to sign contracts with all these interested parties but, as Anna concisely expressed it, our vision of liberating this data was too huge for us to manage on our own. We agreed that the best thing would be if Google were to steal our ideas, because they did not charge users for their services.

In 2006, barely three years after my first presentation to the heads of Swedish industries, I was invited to give my first TED Talk. Anna and Ola had actually been invited a year earlier to what was at the time a secret conference for handpicked delegates and which had not yet put a single video on YouTube. But the TED Talk people refused on principle to pay airfares, trying instead to persuade Anna and Ola what a huge honor it was to be invited at all. To which they had replied: "Sorry, but we can't afford the flights."

Before my first TED presentation, I phoned Anna and Ola to discuss the content.

"What about sword swallowing?" I asked, referring to a party trick of mine.

"No, don't do that," Ola advised. "Run the chimp test and then show them the visuals."

It was an incredible success. I was even on the front page of the *San Francisco Chronicle*.

The following year I was invited to talk at TED again and, true to habit, I phoned Anna and Ola to ask their advice: "What have I got to show them now?"

"Nothing new, so you had better swallow a sword or two," Ola said.

The actor Meg Ryan had a front-row seat. She cheered loudly and jumped up and down when I pulled the sword from my throat and bowed to the audience. I still regard Meg Ryan's cheering as one of my greatest triumphs.

An unassuming-looking man with a long fringe was hovering quietly among the many people who wanted to speak to me after the talk. He turned out to be Larry Page, one of the founders of Google. Unlike most of the other attendees, he had realized right away that I was unlikely to have written the code for my bubble graphs myself. I told him about Anna and Ola, who were promptly invited to Google headquarters along with the programmers working with them at Gapminder, the not-for-profit foundation we had founded. Once installed at Google, they would be able to turn Anna's vision of democratic access to official statistics into reality. The Gapminder Foundation sold the moving-bubble source code to Google and for three years, Anna and Ola worked in the company's Silicon Valley building. Their goal was to create and shape Google Public Data, an application that makes it much easier to find and display statistics.

The proceeds of the sale meant that I finally dared to leave academia. In 2007, I severed almost all links with scientific research, keeping just 10 percent of my post at the Karolinska Institute and devoting 90 percent of my working time to Gapminder. My title there was "edutainer." I employed a new team and we started to put short films up on YouTube.

Over the years that followed, my office was flooded with invitations to lecture all over the world. The pressure was such that I had to engage an assistant. I was constantly asked to speak at conferences, of which some were recurring events and others were

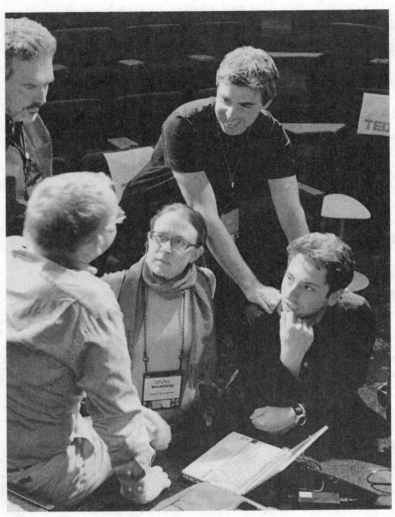

With the founders of Google

one-offs. The latter included a US State Department get-together in Washington DC, where I addressed the foreign affairs specialists with a talk I called "Let my data set change your mindset."

One day, an email arrived from Melinda Gates: would I attend a conference in New York focusing on the United Nations' developmental goals and especially on child mortality. I agreed, of course.

When you are asked to give a talk, you must first make sure you are clear about one thing: what precisely is my subject? Next, you must work out how to illustrate it and what is the best way to display the material. What do I want my audience to remember? I left for New York without having made up my mind about any of this.

My assistant and I arrived, as planned, a day early. I like being in place in good time and to then prepare thoroughly up to the very last minute—it helps me to memorize what I want to say. I always want access to the space to get an idea of the layout and familiarize myself with things like where my laptop will go and where the cable should run. These technical details matter very much to me. Many speakers cannot be bothered and leave their slides in the hands of someone else. I never do. The timing is much better if you are responsible for pressing the button. It gives your talk the pace it needs.

The night before the conference began, I had been invited to a dinner in a restaurant in lower Manhattan, south of UN headquarters.

I was a little uncertain about what to wear. I knew that Graça Machel would be present. She had been the minister of education in Mozambique during the years Agneta and I were there. At the time, she had been married to the president of Mozambique. These days, she was married to Nelson Mandela. Melinda Gates would also be at the dinner.

I chose a jacket but no tie. In my bag, I carried something very precious to me: my daughter Anna's school notepad, carrying the logo of the Mozambican Ministry of Education. My arrival at the restaurant was overwhelming: I had been seated in a central position, next to Graça Machel, with Melinda Gates facing me.

The conversation that evening was quiet but profound and witty, especially the exchanges between Melinda and Graça. They discussed all the great issues of international development. I joined in now and then but mostly listened as these two giants of world policy talked about girls' rights to education, access to contraception, distribution of vaccines in rural areas, the furthering of democratic governance, and whether social development must be achieved before political change is possible—and, in every context, what the UN could do and what the Bill & Melinda Gates Foundation could do. I was fascinated by the way they talked. They were obviously close friends, almost like sisters. Having met so often, and sharing the same values, they knew each other's projects in detail.

Both were deeply concerned about the issues surrounding access to contraception. Melinda felt that the matter should be seen not in terms of human rights but as an intervention in support of family life—for one thing, people grasp that family life will be easier if the children are not born too close together. Graça saw the question from a South African perspective: there, arguing in favor of using contraception was less controversial than in Mozambique, which had experienced extreme poverty so recently. For me, it was a privilege to listen as people with the capacity to make a difference in the world peacefully discuss what best to do next.

Every now and again the two women asked me questions. Among other things, I told them about how to measure child mortality. I described how you had to select a representative female population from the country in question and then arrange for qualified interviewers to ask them about their lives. The questions were probing: for example, how had life been for them during the last few years, had they lost children and, if so, how. This approach enabled us to investigate child mortality in depth.

Graça and Melinda listened attentively and asked me about some critical issues. I told them there was no doubt that most African countries were developing in the right direction because the evidence was there in the form of decreasing child mortality.

Toward the end of the evening, when I felt that we had been getting on very well, I decided it was now or never.

"I would like to show you something. And to thank you," I said to Graça. Melinda peered over the table to see what I had in my hand. I pulled out Anna's school notebook. I spoke about our time in Mozambique from 1979 to 1981 and explained that our daughter had been to school there. Graça Machel's eyes grew wide. "Did you meet my husband?"

"No, but I heard a speech he gave in Nampula," I said.

The notebook caused quite a stir. Everyone wanted to have a look.

"It was the education minister who saw to it that my daughter went to school," I said, while the notebook was handed around the table.

As I walked back through Manhattan that evening I made little elated leaps. Talking with these two women had given me such a high.

The dinner stayed with me as the greatest memory of the trip. It had humbled me. My preconceived notion had been that people in high places were shallow and egotistical. I had thought ill of them, in general, and expected arrogance. Instead, I had met wise, thoughtful and kind individuals.

That dinner conversation also taught me how important personal contacts always are, even at the most elevated social levels. It was an insight that was strengthened every time I attended the World Economic Forum in Davos, an annual event where the power brokers of the world meet to discuss the big issues of the future.

It has grown into the world's largest assembly of people who hold power—those active in industry, economics, and finance as well as politicians, heads of state, representatives of international organizations including the UN and organizations such as Amnesty, leading media figures, and academic experts in global issues.

Davos is an ordinary-looking Alpine town with a modest railway station. It had snowed that morning and as Agneta and I pulled our wheeled suitcases along I slipped and slithered on the steep, icy street.

Before long, I found myself seated in a small meeting room, listening to a minister for the environment from an EU country. He was in an accusatory mood:

"The bulk of the world's carbon dioxide emissions come from China, India, and the other developing economies, and projections show they are rising at a rate that will cause very dangerous climate change. China already releases more carbon dioxide into the atmosphere than the USA, and India releases more than Germany."

The minister was a member of the group of politicians and industrialists discussing climate change at Davos in January 2007. His statement about the CO_2 emissions from China and India was made in a neutral, unemotional tone, as if his view was purely factual. I scanned the small meeting room: Europeans and Americans were seated along one side of the table while delegates from the rest of the world, including India and China with their rapidly growing economies, were lined up along the other side. The Chinese civil servant kept staring straight ahead but his shoulders were drawn up and his neck seemed somehow locked as he listened to what the EU minister had to say. His Indian counterpart was leaning forward and waving to catch the moderator's attention.

When the Indian minister was called upon to speak, he stood calmly for a moment. He wore an elegant navy-blue turban and a dark gray suit. In silence, he looked around the table at each of the other countries' representatives, gazing at the CEO of one of the largest oil companies for a little longer than the rest. As one of India's most senior civil servants, he had many years of experience as an expert advisor to the World Bank and the IMF. After his brief but effective silence, he made a sweeping gesture toward the "wealthy" side of the table.

"We are in a delicate situation. That we are here at all is the fault of your countries, the wealthiest in the world! You fired your economies with coal and have been burning oil for centuries. *Your* activities—no one else's—have brought us all to the brink of a major climate crisis," he said loudly and aggressively, breaking all diplomatic codes.

Then his body language changed abruptly. He pressed the palms of his hands together in front of his chest in an Indian greeting, bowing to the shocked delegates from the West.

"But we forgive you because you did not know what you were doing."

The words were spoken in a near-whisper. The audience was silent. There was a giggle from somewhere in the back. A few people exchanged anxious smiles.

The Indian minister straightened up again, stared at his opponents and wagged his finger at them.

"From today, we will base our calculations on CO_2 emissions *per capita*."

I was so impressed by the sharpness of his analysis that I can't remember the reactions of others in the room. Over the years, I had become horrified at the way blame for causing climate change had been systematically heaped on India and China. The basis has been their total emissions, even though both countries have much larger populations than other countries. I had always thought it was a silly argument, analogous to stating that obesity was a more serious issue in China than in the USA because China's total body mass was the bigger of the two. Given the huge differences in population size, it is pointless to speak of "total emissions per country." Sweden, with ten million inhabitants, could by that logic get away with vastly increased CO_2 emissions per capita because there are so few of us.

What the Indian civil servant expressed in public was something that had worried me for years. Is this really how they think, the men and women in power? But the way he said it made me hope that the restructuring of the world was on its way.

It is interesting to give lectures for company staff and focus on what they feel really matters. Sometimes I use links to my own past—for instance, to my grandma, who washed clothes in a laundry tub in a cement trough while dreaming of a washing machine.

I had been invited to give a talk to the management of a well-known white goods company. The CEO wanted me to demonstrate the world's demographic and economic development and go on to explore the worldwide need for cookers, fridges, and washing machines.

I began with a simple display of how income distribution related to population health, pointing out that people become healthier first and that economic growth follows later. This progress means that today we can make qualified guesses about where development might take off, given a sufficiently good economic policy.

"Asia will be the next enormous marketplace. Latin America and the Middle East as well, but Africa will follow later. For you, expansion in Asia is what matters just now."

Someone asked, "What do they want there, would you say?"

"You make electric cookers, mostly, but often gas is the cheaper fuel in poorer countries. A fridge is probably what households will invest in first; they're much valued, especially in warm climates. But your firm makes expensive goods and people with lower incomes need cheaper things. I don't know what you feel about that.

"Have you talked to your own relatives?" I went on. "Have you ever asked the oldest woman in the family how she felt when the washing machine was installed?"

I pointed at 1952 on the graph displayed behind me. "*Here* is when Swedish families got their first washing machines. We were then at the stage China is at today. Imagine the market—1.3 billion people."

A washing machine is a product that many people in the world would love to own. Imagine that! If you could make washing-machine ownership match mobile-phone ownership, which has spread worldwide.

"What is lacking is a technological breakthrough. The old types of washing machine use too much water, and that will not sell in densely populated Asian countries. Add to this the problem of using detergents and other chemicals, and don't forget the demands on the electricity supply."

They listened. "How will you deal with these problems?" I asked. "Can you think up something as smart as the mobile phone? Once you do, you can access billions of customers. This isn't about 'corporate social responsibility'; it's about your future profits! Unless you get on with redesigning your product, you will lose the leading position in the marketplace."

The arguments inside the corporation became clear: opposing sides wanted either to hang on to old market shares in the West or try out simpler models and gain more customers in new markets. I have rarely seen so distinctly the difference facts can make.

I had spoken to them using the same facts as I had shown to the UN and aid organizations. But I presented them from the producers' point of view. I had just scratched the surface of their outdated view of the world.

In 2011, when our children had grown up and moved out and three decades had passed since we had lived in Mozambique, we decided to return. After flying from Maputo we rented a car in

Nampula and drove toward Nacala. On the way, we passed the place where I had almost died in a car accident. We stopped and stared. It looked just the same: grass and mud. But, as soon as we entered the outskirts of Nacala, we started noticing changes. The town had expanded into the countryside with large industrial sites surrounded by nicely painted walls. A truck swung out onto the road in front of us. It was loaded to the top with colorful, patterned foam-rubber mattresses wrapped in transparent plastic. Ah, at last, I thought. At last people can make love on something soft rather that hard-trodden dirt floors. At last, modernization. That truck seemed symbolic. The port of Nacala had grown to be the industrial city we had hoped it would become. But the really amazing moment for us was returning to the hospital.

We parked on the sloping road leading down into the center. We recognized all the hospital buildings, except one: it was tiny and looked like a small kiosk. The door was covered in posters. One of them showed a man hitting a woman, with a cross through the scene. The door stood open and we peeped inside. We saw a man busy entering things on paper, seated at a dark wooden desk. A fragile-looking, plainly dressed woman of about twenty-five was standing in front of him, wearing flip-flops. Her eyes were frightened.

"Please excuse us. We're disturbing you," we said cautiously.

"Not at all, don't worry," the nurse said. Then he turned to the woman and asked her if she minded if he chatted to us for a while.

We introduced ourselves, explaining that we had worked in the hospital thirty years ago. The nurse, who was probably not yet thirty, said he had heard that foreign doctors had worked there once upon a time. His job, he told us, was to look after the rights of women.

"I help women to take crimes against them to court. I take care of inheritance claims as well, and prepare statements to be given to the police," he said.

We were utterly taken aback. When we had worked in Nacala the level of violence toward women had been grotesque. It is often the case in extremely poor communities, and no one had seemed ready to change it. Now, with basic healthcare being provided, the system had moved on to attacking gender-based crime and defending women's rights. The nurse gave us a small information brochure.

The old building that had housed the outpatient clinic in our time still performed the same function but had now been improved with a veranda running along the front. The shade was a good idea. At one end was a smaller building for the expanding dental service.

The district where I had worked in 1980 had at that time never been served by more than two doctors. Now it was looked after by sixteen medically qualified people and a new hospital had been built. The hospital manager was the most clinically experienced of the doctors working there, a highly qualified and competent Mozambican gynecologist.

In the reception area, we told a nurse that we had worked in the hospital thirty years ago. We showed her a photo of the staff from 1980 and soon a small cluster of people formed around us to have a look. They recognized people, laughing delightedly and commenting on who had died and who had been good-looking in their youth. And to our enormous surprise and delight one of the nurses recognized one of our old assistant nurses, Mama Rosa, and called her on her mobile phone. That was how we later were able to meet some of our old co-workers and share a lunch together.

A nurse showed us round the antenatal clinic linked to the childcare center, where twenty proudly expectant women were sitting in the waiting room. All were nicely dressed. It is what pregnancy feels like in Africa—you are proud and pleased to be pregnant and to attend the social event that is a visit to the antenatal clinic.

What had been the outpatient reception in our time was now a specialized area for patients with HIV and AIDS. It was staffed by two nurses and a doctor. The doctor wore a crisp white coat and was seated at a glass-topped desk. When he heard that his post had been mine thirty years ago, we hugged.

That doctor was now responsible for primary care in the town. He gave me an overview of the pattern of disease. I listened in silence. Later, Agneta pointed out it was ages since I had shut up for an entire half hour.

He had given us a comprehensive understanding of how disease was distributed in his district. They still had problems with childhood infections, and the widespread availability of mosquito nets had not eliminated malaria cases. And, of course, there was pneumonia and diarrhea as well as victims of traffic accidents and other minor and major injuries.

"I assume it was just the same when you were here," he said.

Agneta asked about the child and adolescent psychiatry services. Did they see much ADHD (attention deficit hyperactivity disorder)?

"Yes, we do. It's tragic. We see them coming in for minor surgery." The doctor sighed.

He told us that the new medicines for treating ADHD were too expensive, and psychologists seemed unable to help these children. Their diagnosis meant that they got into trouble—climbing on buildings and trees, hurting themselves falling off, or being beaten up. And then they came in to have wounds stitched.

The thoughtful doctor went on to tell us that he did not work shifts in the hospital as I had done. Also, another doctor was responsible for the rural catchment area. In the 1970s, that had been just another part of my job. His post carried about a third of the workload that mine had but, even so, his load was heavy. He also mentioned that he had hoped to buy a house on the coast but had been too late. The property prices had already risen so much that he could not afford to buy a site with a sea view.

As we left, I was full of admiration and deep respect.

The new hospital had been built a little farther away, high up above the town, on a spacious site with room for expansion. There was an ambulance driveway to an emergency entrance. The morning routine was like that of a Swedish hospital: before the visit to the wards, the day began with an X-ray session and a brief review of the emergency patients from the night.

Because of the infection risk, you were allowed to put your ruck-sack only on a chair and not on the floor. The delivery suite had a tiled floor that could be washed and to avoid dirt being brought in, the staff wore indoor shoes. These days, dehydrated children in Nacala were put on intravenous drips, just as my pediatrician friend had insisted should be the case thirty years earlier.

This Mozambique was not like the country we had lived in. This is not to say that everything was perfect—far from it. But everything had moved forward.

There were still extremely poor areas to the north of Nacala, where two junior medics worked alone, serving a large popula-tion. The size of their task became clear when we heard of the thirteen-year-old girl who had become pregnant. When she was about to give birth, the girl, whose pelvis was too narrow for childbirth, had become extremely ill. She had been transported to the hospital from her remote part of the district—a northern area from where, in my days, we saw no patients at all. On the way to Nacala, the crisis point was reached and her uterus burst. She not only lost the baby but had to have her torn uterus surgi-cally removed, meaning she would never be able to have children. Agneta and I knew only too well what it means when a very young girl begins a home delivery and her body gives up. The message was clear: in some parts of the district, the poverty was no better than in our time, but *here*, in town, things had improved.

The staff was exceedingly curious and keen to talk with me. They were very aware that some aspects of the health service were still insufficient and hoped I would want to stay. Lack of special-

At my desk, then and now

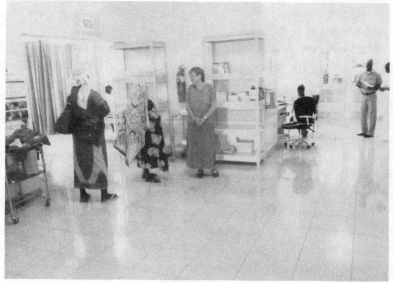

The clinic, then and now

ization was one obstacle to continued development. There was a role for me, I felt—in my thirties, I had been the doctor who tried to learn from the nurses, but now, in my sixties, I could be useful by training specialists. The young doctors had been to medical school in the capital and had their degrees, but lacked the specialist skills you acquire during the years as a junior doctor under the guidance of senior and experienced specialists.

During my two years in Nacala in the late 1970s, I never diagnosed a case of type 1 diabetes. The patients all died before they saw a doctor. Now, the medics were having to learn to cope with such previously unseen diseases. During the ward round that evening, we witnessed the changing times in the shape of a twenty-one-year-old woman.

She was extremely thin, as anyone is with advanced, untreated diabetes. Her entire body language expressed alarm. As the ward-round staff stood talking to one another, she seemed to expect them to turn to her and tell her she would die.

Diabetes begins with frequent peeing and weight loss, followed by hyperventilation, loss of consciousness, and then death, unless insulin is given in time. The progression can be fast, sometimes as short as one week.

I tried to say something soothing, as one does when standing by a hospital bed. The Mozambican doctors stood to my left and right and I told them about her condition, as I myself had once been taught about treating diabetics by more experienced medics at Hudiksvall hospital back in 1975.

We spent that whole week in and around Nacala. It was moving to see again the colleagues from the two most intensive years of clinical practice of our lives. We noted the growth of the local economy but also the huge challenges that still remained.

Mama Rosa, the assistant nurse from the maternity ward thirty years ago, arranged a lunch for us at a restaurant close to the marketplace. Papa Enrique, to whom I had once given my spare spectacles, was now almost blind and needed help with his food. His grandson had brought him on his motorbike. It was unclear whether Enrique recalled anything of his past life and it was difficult to talk with him as his hearing was not the best, but we did all we could to try to explain who we were. Seeing them all again made me almost tearful.

And now, at last, I had a chance to apologize to Ahmed.

Ahmed had been our hospital cleaner. I used to walk round inspecting the whole hospital, even the toilets. I lost my temper if anything looked dirty. Everywhere had to be clean.

One morning, the toilets were filthy, not even flushed properly. I was outraged and shouted: "Where is Ahmed?"

"He isn't in yet," someone said.

"What, not in yet? It's quarter to nine already!"

"We don't know what's happened."

"Can't someone go and fetch him?"

"But maybe we should just wait—"

I interrupted, speaking more loudly: "Someone should go and get him here, now."

An hour later, Ahmed stood outside my door, shaking.

"*Senhor Doktor*, I am very sorry that I'm late. My son died last night."

My expression did not change. "Is that so? What did he die from?"

"Measles."

"Why didn't you see that he was vaccinated?"

Ahmed's first-born son had died. His home had been taken over by the wake but there I was, telling him off for being late and then for not having had his child vaccinated. It was a dreadful moment to remember and also an indication of how much pressure I had been under, like everyone who worked there at the time.

Ahmed did not want to discuss that episode, and so the talk returned to everyday events and old anecdotes.

We drove past our old house and both felt very touched to see what was still stuck to the back door. There had been a break-in while we lived there and the thieves smashed the window in the kitchen door. I repaired it by nailing the lid of a wooden box sent from Sweden. Our family had packed it full of food from home. The address label on the lid read "To Doctor Hans Rosling, Nacala," and the text was still visible thirty years later.

It was striking that those two years, which had meant so much to us, had mattered so little in Nacala. We left the town and were still shocked by the hopelessness of the apparently stagnant life in the most remote villages, where little or nothing had changed. At the same time, we had been encouraged by the inspiring young Mozambicans we had met.

On the last day of our return visit to Mozambique, we had been invited by a seventy-six-year-old lady to take afternoon tea. She had been born in the USA but had become a Mozambican citizen long ago. She shared with us her very realistic, factual take on her country's development. Her views were based on a deep understanding of what building the nation of Mozambique had meant. Her name was Janet Mondlane.

Agneta and I had met Janet in Sweden in the autumn of 1968. She had been one of our very first guests for supper in our shared student apartment.

Janet was born in the 1930s in Illinois. At the age of seventeen, she attended a talk at the local church in Geneva, Wisconsin, given by Eduardo Mondlane, about the future of Africa. Eduardo had grown up in rural Mozambique and had just arrived to begin his university studies in the USA when he and Janet met. They married a couple of years later and had three children together before they moved to Dar es Salaam in Tanzania. Eduardo became the leader of FRELIMO, the Mozambican liberation movement, and organized its headquarters there in neighboring Tanzania. Unlike Europe's other colonial powers, Portugal's fascist regime had no intention of giving up its African colonies.

While in Tanzania, Janet Mondlane took on responsibility for running an education center to help Mozambicans in exile. She had come to Sweden to raise money for her project. I remember well how surprised Agneta and I had been by her conversation over dinner in 1968. She spoke like a true Mozambican, even though she had never set foot in the country. She impressed us, just as her husband had done when I met him a year or so earlier, with her ability to think ahead, beyond independence and far into the future. She was setting up courses for teachers who would one day educate the next generation of teachers in the independent Mozambique.

Eduardo was killed only a year later. After the 1975 day of independence, as the widow of the country's first leader, Janet Mondlane moved to Maputo, its capital. We never met her while we were living there but now we were invited for tea. We had a friend in common, Julie Cliff, professor of epidemiology in Maputo. It was Julie who arranged for us to see Janet, forty-three years after we last met.

Her home was in a beautiful spot on the top of a hill in the center of the city. You could see the harbor entrance from her windows. Her first-floor flat was modest, though. We recognized her at once. Her smile was as charming as it had been so long ago.

"Welcome," she said. "At last, I have a chance to return your invitation."

After a quick tour of her home, when we were seated on her sofa, I simply had to ask her about the past: "Do you really remember having supper with us in 1968, in our tiny student apartment?"

She laughed happily and slapped her palms against her legs.

"I sure do! I don't remember what we ate, but I remember you served the meal in the kitchen," she said.

Agneta and I looked at each other, thinking the same thing: our guest had remembered the cultural oddity of serving dinner in the kitchen even though our sitting room had enough space for a formal dining table. Janet quickly read our thoughts and took our hands in hers.

"I also remember how young we all were, and how much at home I felt in your company. You were so interested in our struggle for independence," she said. "But tell me: do you think Mozambique has changed since you were working here thirty years ago?"

She nodded agreement when I mentioned the greater number of doctors in Nacala, and she was even more pleased to hear Agneta speak about the new primary schools in most suburbs and villages, and how senior school classes had been added where there was only junior teaching before. We had both been delighted and impressed to see teenage boys and girls streaming into newly built school buildings painted in lovely colors.

Then we had to mention our despair at seeing the extreme poverty that still existed in the left-behind villages, and the tone became more subdued. We asked Janet about politics, governance and funding. Was aid money used in the best possible way to further economic growth? How corrupt were the community leaders really? And the question that Janet often had to deal with: if your husband were alive, would corruption be less extensive?

She was very composed and serious when she answered our questions, like a friend sharing something very important with us.

"Being head of state in one of Africa's poorest countries is very difficult: possibly the toughest, most challenging job in the world. People are looking to you to meet many and varied needs—from those who live in extreme poverty to members of your own extended family. So many individuals depend on you. You have been helped by them through your life and now they expect you to reciprocate.

"Honestly, I can't be sure how my husband would have turned out as president. Maybe neither better nor worse than the presidents that followed him. And I think our current one, Armando Guebuza, is doing well."

Janet explained what she had observed as Mozambique was being built. The vision she and her husband had shared when they returned to Africa fifty years ago had now become reality. The former colony was now a relatively stable, independent country with elected presidents in lawful succession. The people were now much better educated. The university in the capital, named after Janet's husband, not only trained teachers and other professionals but was developing its own areas of research specialization.

"It all takes time. Looking from outside, you tend to see our failures. There are still so many serious problems that obscure how far we have come," she said. "What you say about Nacala fits with what I see—lots of progress but still so much more to do."

Then she became very serious. She put down her cup of tea and cake to free her hands so that she could gesture to emphasize her message.

"Considering where Mozambique started, and how far we aim to go, thirty years is not a very long time." Development must be allowed to take its time.

Some things, however, cannot wait. One case in point: a deadly virus able to cross oceans. My most terrifying and challenging job began in 2014, when ebola broke out in western Africa.

7

Ebola

Fear of ebola hit me hard one day in September 2014. That afternoon, I had spotted on Twitter an article about ebola, published in the *New England Journal of Medicine*, the USA's most prestigious medical-research journal. The authors of the article were Chris Dye, Director of Strategy at the WHO, and his team.

Their research included a graph that made me freeze with dread: it showed a steep increase, week by week, in the number of new cases of ebola during the past month. The expected number of new cases for the weeks to come was also plotted on the graph. The spread of the epidemic would accelerate unless something drastic was done to stop the outbreak. I remember even reading some of the article out loud to myself.

The previous evening I had come home from making a presentation in Portugal and the following morning I was due to leave for Switzerland to make another. Despite this, I stayed up for a long time, absorbed by this crucial study. I had been aware of the ebola outbreak since February, when it was first mentioned in the news, and since August I had started to be seriously worried about the epidemic in western Africa. Yet during these past months, what I had felt was more a professional concern.

Chris Dye's research team had used ebola data from the start of the epidemic up to September 14 to calculate an estimate of the expected number of cases per day as far ahead as early November. It was the way the line representing their predictions curved ever more steeply upward that was so frightening: the number of new cases per day had doubled every third week until mid-September, and their analysis indicated that this would continue if the response to the epidemic was not fast and effective enough.

Already by the beginning of September, people were dying in the streets of Monrovia, Liberia's capital city, something that had not happened in modern times except during wartime or because of a natural disaster. So many people had fallen ill so quickly. The field medical facilities had soon run out of beds, and many patients never got treatment.

That graph predicted what would happen if the number of new cases continued to double every third week. Nine weeks later, at the start of November, the number of new patients per day would be not twice as many, not four times as many, but eight times as many as now.

If the cases increased at this rate, Monrovia, the place likely to be the most severely affected, would soon be paralyzed. The progression is called exponential growth or, if you prefer, explosive growth. The numbers suggested that, on average, each patient would infect two healthy individuals and each of them would become ill enough within a few weeks to infect two more, and so on. But it was not the figures in themselves that triggered my sense of fear, but imagining the situation in Monrovia in November, if this exponential growth of the disease continued unchecked. Liberia would sink into even greater chaos than during the recently ended civil war. Many would rush to leave the country. That would be catastrophic, because then the spread of the disease would become international and utterly unpredictable.

These fears changed our priorities at Gapminder that year. What could we do to help? We produced informative videos explaining the threat. Our focus was on attempting to explain what would happen if the number of new cases doubled every third week. Our short films were viewed by millions in just a few days.

The ebola outbreak had so far been almost totally confined to three small countries in West Africa: Guinea, Sierra Leone, and Liberia. Why then had fear of ebola grown so fast in Europe and North

America during 2014? Because the deadly virus can be transported across borders and oceans inside a human body. Any infected individual who traveled elsewhere was liable to infect others wherever they ended up. The dread of the disease was, of course, heightened by the fact that there was still no effective treatment.

Six months earlier, at the end of March 2014, I had taken note in passing that the WHO had announced the spread of ebola from Guinea to Liberia. Little did I know that six months later I would have a desk of my own in Liberia's Ministry of Health in Monrovia and that I would be working as the "Deputy Director of ebola Surveillance." If, in addition, someone had told me that, because of ebola, this would be the first year that I would not celebrate Christmas and New Year with my wife and my family, it would have sounded like a bad joke. As it happened I ended up celebrating an unforgettable Christmas that year in the company of Luke Bawo, my roommate and boss in Liberia. Just before I left Liberia, I was honored by being accorded traditional chieftain status and given the title "Chief Tanue."

It was only later in the autumn of 2014 that the reality dawned on me: I had to cancel or postpone all engagements and offer my services to the battle against ebola. Experts like me should have understood the extent of the danger earlier. Most of us took our time to grasp the urgency of the epidemic and so, too, did the rest of the world. The handful of expert epidemiologists and tropical-disease specialists who did see what was coming worked for the WHO and did not have the necessary kind of budget to take action.

Why did we fail in this way? We had for some time been observing several outbreaks of ebola, all in faraway African countries. During the second half of 2013 and the spring of 2014, the virus had been on the move from the remote highlands of rural Guinea to equally isolated regions of Liberia and Sierra Leone, but the world did not care. None of the outbreaks had spread to capital cities—that is, the infection had never come close to sites of government or to international airports.

Before long, though, there were cases in Conakry and Monrovia, the capitals of Guinea and Liberia respectively.

Public health professionals, and that includes me, should have reacted more quickly when cases of ebola started to spread to large cities with extensive slums. I blame myself, particularly, because I am not just any professor in global health: for decades, my research focused on epidemics in remote parts of rural Africa. The insight that ebola had the potential to become a major global threat if the infection spread to a capital city with a large slum population and an international airport was one I had already shared with most scientists working in this field. And now it had actually happened.

On August 8, 2014, the WHO declared that the ebola epidemic had become an acute danger to health on an international scale. Now, finally, everyone sat up and took notice. The alarm spread. Foreign investment stopped, at first leading to counterproductive measures such as flight cancelations and attempts to isolate the afflicted countries. Eventually, resources were diverted to control the disease in western Africa.

The worldwide fear felt at the time was completely justified but it surfaced too late. By then, all we could do was make up for lost time.

It was October 10. We were in the government building in Stockholm. Eugene Bushayija looked straight at me. He was clearly very worried; "No one understands what should be done about the ebola outbreak in Monrovia," he said.

Eugene worked for Médecins Sans Frontières. We had just come to the end of a meeting with Swedish government officials and academics about what Sweden could contribute to stop the epidemic. Now, only the two of us were left in the meeting room and we found ourselves agreeing that nobody seemed to know exactly what was going on in western Africa.

Eugene went on: "MSF treatment centers are admitting as many ill patients as they have the capacity to treat. The majority test positive for ebola. But we're not running the only facilities and because MSF is independent of the government, we can no longer be sure of the overall picture. Still, our center in Monrovia alone registered more confirmed cases than are shown in this week's WHO report."

I was very well aware that hard clinical work in field hospitals was unsuitable for someone of my age, but I felt there must be something I could do.

Ten days after the meeting in Stockholm, in late October 2014, I was at my new desk in Monrovia. I had brought a couple of suitcases full of everything I thought I might need: a laptop, a printer, a projector, spare memory sticks, and—not least—appropriate clothing. At first, Agneta had reservations. Did I really have to go? Was I desperate to prove to myself and others how brave I still was? We talked about my plan, and Agneta came to the conclusion that I probably could make a difference. I had her full support.

I spent the time on the plane reading up on ebola. Before landing, I prepared to protect myself against exposure to infection. What would the airport be like? I ought to have brought disinfectant wipes to clean my suitcase, I thought, as my head filled with all the likely and unlikely routes of infection. A friendly woman from the Swedish embassy picked me up at the airport and drove me to the Grand Hotel, where the embassy had booked a room for me. Before entering the hotel, I was shown a disinfectant routine: I had to wash my hands in a bucket of chlorinated water. The bucket was on a stool and on the floor next to it was a plastic basin also with chlorinated water for me to step into with my shoes on.

The hotel seemed to have been recently built. The lobby was an elegant space, with tall, freshly painted pale-yellow walls and pillars of dark-red stone supporting the high ceiling. To the right, I spotted an ATM and two small shops. The smiling receptionist handed me the key to a third-floor room.

I have never been so appreciative of a high-class, spotlessly clean hotel room as I was then. Yet the risks were still too great. I washed and cleaned myself as carefully as I have ever done, then I wiped all the wardrobe shelving with chlorhexidine-soaked wipes and obsessively placed my clothing in piles that did not touch the walls. Then I cleaned the desk and the outside of my suitcases with more disinfectant wipes. Finally, I went to bed, slept restlessly and dreamed I was running a fever. Fear of infection stayed with me throughout my time in Monrovia, but after a week or two these preparations had turned into a daily routine that I hardly noticed.

During my first day in Monrovia, I was given an overview of the local response to the epidemic. Everywhere was full of frantic activity. Experts were crowded into small rooms with maps of Liberia on the walls. I was ushered in and out of tall office buildings, always stopping at the entrance for the compulsory washing of hands and shoes in chlorinated water. Introductions went easily at the American office run by the federal Centers for Disease Control and Prevention (CDC) because the staff recognized me from my TED talks. They were extremely keen to find out what I was doing in Liberia and surprised to learn that I had come to work for several months as an independent expert.

Liberia's Deputy Chief Medical Officer Tolbert Nyenswah also recognized me when we came across each other in one of the many corridors I wandered along that day. I gave him my Karolinska Institute card and explained that I had been investigating epidemics in poor African countries for almost twenty years, after first working as a district doctor in the public health service in Mozambique.

"In other words, I do understand what shortage of resources can mean," I added.

He nodded, his expression a mixture of surprise and approval. There was no reason he should have known of my background before I went on the lecture circuit. I bent down to get a letter from my bag.

"I have brought with me a letter to your president, Ellen Johnson Sirleaf. It is from the Royal Academy of Sciences in Stockholm. May I deliver it through you?"

It had been beautifully handwritten on the academy's thick correspondence paper. The permanent secretary, Staffan Normark, as a representative not only of the academy but also the entire international scientific establishment, was apologizing that research into ebola had not advanced further than it had at present.

This had troubled me, too. We, a group of experts on international public health, had earlier compiled a list of seventeen diseases needing further research into treatment, and presented it to the pharmaceutical companies. Ebola was included in the list. Because the research has not been carried out, simple test methods, vaccines, and disease-specific medication were not available.

Tolbert's face was serious as he read the brief letter. Then he sighed a little, looked up at me with screwed-up eyes and, after a moment's silence, said to me: "Thank you. We have never been addressed in these terms before. The president will appreciate this apology."

In another corridor I was introduced to Liberia's ultra-efficient deputy minister of health. He told me: "Please join us tomorrow at the coordination meeting. It's on the ground floor and starts at nine. I will introduce you to our own leaders of the disease response and also the experts from abroad. You are very welcome here."

My admiration and respect for Tolbert Nyenswah's outstanding leadership ability, and the calm, thoughtful way in which he managed the entire response to the ebola outbreak, would continue to grow during the months I had the privilege of working under him.

Back in my cool, air-conditioned hotel room after my first day, I felt anxious about infection in my sweaty clothes. I wiped my bag down with paper napkins soaked in hand-cleaning alcohol. I stripped, wiped my belt with more napkins, and put all my clothes in the laundry basket. I showered. The whole cleansing process, which included paying extra careful attention to my nails, took more than half an hour. Wearing only a clean pair of underpants, I folded back the bedspread, blanket, and top sheet and lay down on the bed.

Lying there, I reflected on my first day. It had worked out unexpectedly well but I felt doubtful nonetheless. Would I achieve what I had set out to do? I also felt a little ashamed about my ultra-intensive cleaning routine, but it had calmed me, too, and would become a soothing ritual that I carried out each day.

I rested for a little longer and then took the elevator to the top-floor restaurant, had an excellent buffet dinner and rounded it off by sipping a Coca-Cola beneath the black, star-studded sky. The tropical night was warm up there on the roof terrace. A grant from the Wallenberg Foundations, which fund research deemed beneficial to Sweden, had made it possible for me to stay in the best hotel in Monrovia. I resolutely silenced my critical conscience but told myself sternly: "You shall have to make up for all this by working hard." Back in my room, I fell asleep quickly, but was woken by a nightmare where I fell ill with fever and diarrhea.

"Why does the WHO report say that the current number of confirmed ebola cases in Monrovia is close to zero? It's obviously not true!" I spoke frankly at the following morning's meeting with the staff at the American CDC office.

This had also not escaped Frank Mahoney, one of the world's best, most experienced infection epidemiologists. It had infuriated him and he launched into a systematic account of what he thought were the reasons. Frank was short and a bit overweight, with a crew cut and unshaven chin. He wore an ill-fitting dark jacket with a limp tie. His colleague Joel Montgomery, also a very skilled infection epidemiologist, just as his shirt was a little whiter and his hair a fraction longer than Frank's, spoke more calmly.

Both men thought the problem stemmed somehow from the epidemic surveillance office at the Ministry of Health. Its head was a Liberian called Luke Bawo. Terry Lo, another American epidemiologist, cut into my questions and speculations: "I think you should go to the ministry and chat to him. He's very easy to talk to. I'm working with his group there. Why don't you come along with me after this meeting?"

It was late morning when we set out, and the sun was flooding Monrovia with light. A quarter of an hour later, the car pulled up in front of the health ministry's three-story building of yellowing concrete. Around the car park, filled mostly with white jeeps bearing the ministry's logo, was a high wall of the same discolored concrete.

Before we were allowed into its long corridors, guards at the entrance to the ministry kept watchful eyes on us to check that we followed the chlorinated-water sanitation regime. Terry Lo took me to his office, where people were hard at work at the four desks they had managed to squeeze into the room.

"I'm managing the HISP database," a middle-aged Irishman and WHO staffer said.

"HISP? What is that?" I asked.

They all stared at me, obviously baffled at my failure to recognize the acronym.

"The Health Information System Data."

Just as I was about to start asking questions about the data-entry system, the door was pushed open. The newcomer stepped quickly inside. The swiftness of his movements was amazing because he had a gammy leg that he had to push forward with his hand. No one seemed to notice, though, and he was very much in control of his movements, suggesting that he had coped with his handicap for a long time.

Terry gestured to catch his attention: "Professor Rosling, I'd like to introduce our boss, Luke Bawo."

Luke spoke in a broad, Liberian-accented English, and I had

to strain to follow what soon became a lively conversation. Keen to find out what I was doing there, he asked me some straightforward questions. I said that I wanted very much to contribute to the ministry's efforts to control ebola and added that I was fully financed to work in an independent capacity.

"Trouble is, another desk will hardly fit in here," I finally pointed out.

That was easily dealt with. Quickly, Luke ushered me into the room next door and made a welcoming gesture. It had an air-conditioning unit, a small fridge, and two green-painted metal desks with tops made of brown-speckled plastic. The larger of the two desks was stacked high with piles of paper, boxes and a printer. The smaller one was empty.

Luke pointed at it: "That is your desk."

"Thank you," I said, pleased and surprised. "And whose desk is that?" I asked, indicating the larger one.

"It's mine. You will be based in my room, as the deputy head of ebola surveillance. We can easily share the work between us here. You can have a key of your own, I have a spare. There's room for your bag as well," he said and pointed to a space behind my desk.

He was not being bossy but spoke calmly and pleasantly as if all these things were perfectly natural. Then, his face and voice grew more serious.

"We really need you in Liberia. Will this be all right for you?" he asked, looking deep into my eyes. I liked his unaffected, direct manner but felt quite startled: less than twenty minutes after walking through the front door, I had been offered an official post in the ministry. My thoughts flashed back over how smoothly everything had run, from the immediate reply to my inquiry about a UN secondment to the completion of my preparations in Sweden. I had ended up in the best hotel in town and had gained the best possible impression of the Liberian in charge of the battle against ebola.

Since then, I have reflected on how quickly I made up my mind.

"Yes, it's great. But is it really this simple? Ought we not write an agreement and sign it, both of us?" I asked.

"No need for that," Luke said.

Luke would go on to meet all my expectations of a good boss. We became very close friends and since I couldn't spend that Christmas with my own family, I spent it with his. Within a few days, I had my business cards bearing the ministry logo and a little later I received a gift of several stunning, colorful West African shirts.

"You must stop wearing your pale blue shirts," Luke said. "These will make you look like one of us."

He had a good reason for his gift. Most of the foreign staff employed in the battle against ebola were equipped with T-shirts, vests, and caps bearing the logos or initials of their organizations. My clothes had to show who I was: an official, employed by the Ministry of Health and the government of Liberia.

My role was to work with Luke's staff to compile the figures and write the text of the daily, ten-page report, which Luke then checked and published.

The problem with the report soon became painfully obvious. The staff relied on a database provided by the CDC. The recording routines had functioned well enough during previous ebola outbreaks. In this outbreak, however, the daily number of confirmed cases was much larger than before.

On my first day, I discovered that not every one of the thirteen Liberian country districts provided daily reports. The reason was the irregularity of contact via email and telephone, and the outcome was that a classic error was introduced: the entry "zero" stood for "no new cases," but where there was no report at all it was also entered as "zero." My first intervention was to introduce a "black box" in the table when no report was available, instead of a zero.

Another problem was that getting in touch with the district officials reporting on ebola was done at the personal expense of ministry staff, who had to use their own phones and public phone cards to talk to colleagues in remote regions. The ministerial budget did not stretch to cover all these calls, and the international organizations, with their huge economic resources, had omitted to give telephone cards to key personnel, presumably to "prevent corruption."

It did not take me long to set up a dedicated funding scheme by way of an agreement between Gapminder and the Liberian Ministry of Health. The aim was to provide free telephone cards for members of staff and there was only one restriction: the cards must be used both to contact colleagues, and to call friends and relations around the country every evening, to gather information and pick up on rumors of new cases. The only other, very strict rule was that anyone caught selling "air time" on the cards would be in deep trouble. The phone card fund was financed by minor donations from Swedish philanthropic sources who wanted to contribute to the fight against ebola, and administered by Gapminder. This highly cost-effective and quickly implemented measure was made possible thanks to my position at the ministry and support from The World We Want Foundation, the Jochnick Foundation, and the Anders Wall Foundation.

In August and September 2014, in the weeks running up to the publication of the academic article that finally prompted me to take action, the slums in Monrovia had suffered the world's largest ever outbreak of ebola in a densely populated area. The CDC database had been built to accommodate separate inputs from three sources: first, an examination of the patient at home, second, an examination of the patient on admittance to a treatment facility, and third, the laboratory test results. By the second half of September, a few weeks before I arrived in Monrovia, this system had imploded.

Data collection became impossible because the three-step input requirement presupposed consistent identification of the patient at every stage, by an ID card or similar. One person had to take a note of the examination in the patient's home; next the clinic staff had to report the admission; and, last but not least, when the patient's blood sample had been analyzed in a laboratory, the result had to be added to that individual's data set.

Because Liberians were identified only by name, address, age, and gender, and not by a unique identifying number, minor variations in the spelling of names or errors with house numbers could cause the entire thing to fall apart. It was perfectly possible for the same person to be counted three times. So, of course, no one trusted the figures. That also meant that the laboratories started entering the blood-sample data into their own Excel spreadsheets, which they did not share.

Everyone involved was more or less aware what was going on but no one in an advisory or executive position was prepared to accept the need for drastic change. A simplified reporting system had to be introduced to give the authorities a proper overview of the course of the epidemic. I drew up some new guidelines. As Luke looked through them he appeared worried: "What will the WHO say if we get rid of their format?"

"They will have to put up with it."

As Luke continued to go through my suggestions, I stressed that we had to get the data in order fast, as we had a crisis on our hands. But what foreign agency could I possibly get to work on the huge backlog of lab data?

"I'm going to ask my boss in Stockholm. His name is Ola Rosling and he is actually my son. He is also a very fast Excel data compiler."

The suggestion made Luke beam. Within a few hours, all the laboratory Excel files had been transferred to Ola. He got up early in the morning and began to compile all the test data from a total of 6,582 blood samples. First thing the following morning, I checked my email and found the completed and reliable graphic representation of the number of new cases of ebola. And happily, the graph indicated that the number of confirmed cases was already declining.

* * *

"I've figured out a good solution, I think," Moses Massaquoi said one day at the beginning of December. Moses was a jovial man with an incisive mind. He carried the responsibility for all Liberia's treatment facilities and was one of the country's six leaders of the fight against ebola. What he had devised was a way to deal with an unexpected and rather irksome problem. That morning, a few Liberians and I had lingered after the end of the coordination meeting. I had just shown the latest graph, which showed that the number of new cases in Monrovia was continuing to fall and was now below ten per day.

Moses had also displayed a data set: the five functional treatment facilities in the capital were almost empty—there were six hundred unoccupied beds. The troubling fact was that several international organizations had been slow off the mark with the promised construction of the additional treatment units and now that they had finally been built, they were no longer needed.

"It wouldn't have become a problem if these guys had simply accepted the facts and refrained from carrying out their plans," Moses said and sighed deeply. He turned to Tolbert and explained that, regardless of what we had agreed with the heads of organizations at coordination meetings, foreign ambassadors took it upon themselves to see the president and insist on going ahead with the buildings. Apparently, it was hugely important to have reports of the opening ceremonies shown on television back home.

"It's true, the president is under pressure. What's this smart solution you've cooked up?" Tolbert asked.

"We arrange a solemn ceremony for them. Military choir and music, someone from the ministry on hand to thank the ambassador in front of the entrance. Staff lined up wearing full protective kit. Great TV, right? But we only let them hand over the units to us, not open them for admissions. Not until we've agreed on wider uses for patients with conditions other than ebola."

Everyone grinned broadly at Moses's brilliant idea.

"It could work. I'll have a word with them," Tolbert said, still laughing.

This exchange must not be misunderstood: the overwhelming majority of the international aid organizations made very valuable contributions. It was only when it came to reporting their work for outside audiences that most of them seemed ready to resort to gross manipulations. I assume the main reason was self-preservation, because they had to ensure financial support from their base, be it government grants or public donations. Or perhaps it could be about a particular charity boss securing their position. Whatever the reasons, from the Liberian perspective their behavior was not helpful.

During November, the number of new ebola cases in Liberia fell quickly. The outbreaks in the countryside were brought under control, one after the other. By the end of November, the graph suggested the epidemic could be over before Christmas.

In order to avoid the illusion that we might soon give the all-clear, I re-plotted the graph with the cases shown on a logarithmic scale on the y-axis. It showed that the outbreak would end as it began—following a slow course with fewer and fewer cases but with sudden flare-ups. The success in the fight against ebola had to a large extent been due to the Liberian public having grasped what was needed, like local shops setting up hand-washing areas, and parents keeping children out of school.

During December, work to control the epidemic was marked by the psychological effects of sheer tiredness on the part of the clinical staff. Patients admitted to the nearly empty units were well cared for but the follow-up and, notably, contact-tracing was far from ideal. Data analyses were incomplete as work became routine for most people. It was very important to reset thought patterns—to re-prioritize. The guiding concept should be a phase-change, as I called it, of our main task: with the "fireman phase" completed, the "detective phase" must begin. It meant, among other things, that we registered cases by name rather than by numbers. The tracing of patient contacts must be perfect if this epidemic was ever going to be stopped.

This was why I decided, in the middle of December, to shift half of my work schedule away from epidemiological surveillance at the ministry to a new base in the office of the capital's contact-tracing group. I also organized a "war room," which was used for meetings dealing with the reports that came in every morning to the coordinator of the contact unit. The room was also a workplace for the epidemiologists employed by the international organizations at work in different sectors of the country.

One central task was to mark all cases on a detailed map of the city. Another, equally important one was to indicate on the map where possible contacts lived, as reported by patients. It gave us a citywide overview of the spread of the disease.

As soon as we found out that someone had died from ebola, we would compile a list of all physical contacts that the dead person might have had. During the very first few days after becoming infected, an infected individual was not infectious to others. It was when their symptoms were just becoming noticeable that we needed to isolate them. This was the key to stopping the spread of the virus. We scrutinized the lists and made daily rounds of home visits to find people who might have been close to an ebola patient.

One day, a boy went missing from a family on our list. His mother claimed to have no idea where he was. Actually, she was reluctant to tell us. In cases like this, we turned to Mosoka Fallah, a Liberian with a doctorate in epidemiology, a generous heart, and a sharp brain.

Mosoka went to talk to the woman. She was a single mother because her husband had left her. The boy had been taken away by his dad, she admitted. It happened now and then, and she couldn't stop it. It is typical of the lot of women in poor communities. For one thing, there is no official help—no emergency services to call.

Gently, Mosoka persuaded her to get the boy back. Because she couldn't afford the fares for a journey across the city, Mosoka gave her money and she agreed to go the next day.

Then she looked at the notes in her hand: "I can't use these, such new, crisp notes. It won't help if I crunch them up—he will see they're new all the same."

In the slums, bank notes are worn and tattered because they do the rounds hundreds and hundreds of times. Her former husband would spot straightaway that some wealthy person had given her cash in hand. She was frightened that he would become angry and uncooperative if he thought she was sharing any kind of information about their lives with people he didn't know. Nothing must give her away.

So Mosoka fixed her up with old notes and she brought the boy home the following day. Not only that: because she now trusted Mosoka, she became a contact-tracer for us. Mosoka Fallah had understood that in the fight against epidemics, your mind must encompass a love of humanity as well as spreadsheets.

In the ebola epidemic, it was even more important than usual to empathize with people's needs as well as to think in numbers. Identifying exactly where the numbers of new cases were increasing or decreasing was one of our hardest tasks, and burials created special problems in this regard. We could not understand why, in these extreme conditions, it was still essential to transport a corpse to the home village to be buried.

I remember one such case very well. A grandmother had contracted ebola, quickly became very ill and died. Her family had promised to fulfill her wish to be buried next to her husband. They kept their promise: they washed her body, clothed it in a nice dress and loaded it into a run-down taxi. The cab driver was paid risk money for the trip to the grandmother's home village and the family jumped in next to the body. Granny was buried and ebola was spread to another village. We tried to communicate the precautionary message but often in vain.

It was hard to grasp why it should be so. How could people be so thoughtless? But it was not a matter of being clever or stupid. In the example above, it was all about love for a mother or a grandmother, the heroic woman who had helped her family all her life, perhaps also during the civil war. Was the most important duty to her or to the authorities? For most people, such choices were hard.

We knew we should be offering grants toward burials, and managed to do this toward the end of the epidemic for some cases. People were allowed to decide where to bury their dead but were given a shroud by the Red Cross, a body wrap that left the face exposed. The actual ceremony was conducted with the help of "funeral assistants" in protective clothing, who placed the body in the grave. It worked well as long as the assistants were humane as well as technically well-informed.

"Can I come in?"

There was a gentle knock and a woman put her head round the office door. Her black hair had been plaited into two beautiful, long, thin plaits that framed her face and flowed over her shoulders. I recognized her: Miatta Gbanya, the head of finance in the Ministry of Health who had been appointed deputy leader of the countrywide response to ebola. I invited her in and said that she was always welcome.

"I actually need to have a word with Luke. Do you know where he is?"

I didn't, but expected him back soon because we had the daily report to go through.

This was near the end of November. Because the number of new confirmed cases was definitely shrinking, our days had become less hectic.

"Have a seat, you surely need a few minutes' rest," I said and pulled out a chair for her.

We had discussed official issues on several occasions but it was a privilege to spend a few minutes with the busiest civil servant in charge of ebola control. I knew that Miatta Gbanya grew up during the civil war, trained in nursing, and had joined the work of humanitarian organizations in the Congo and South Sudan. She later went off to Bangladesh to study at its best university and acquired a master's degree in public health.

I admired her a great deal and also had a question for her that I so far had not dared to ask. She seemed in a good mood, so this might be the right moment to satisfy my curiosity.

"I have gathered that the worst time was the month before I arrived at the end of October. What was it like for you then? What was the most difficult thing you had to deal with?"

She looked thoughtful. So many bad things had happened then.

"Perhaps the very worst moment was at the beginning of October. I was on the phone to the States. They had been persuaded to donate extra generously to ebola control measures, but I had to tell them that they were about to make their funding conditional on the wrong things. I had my work mobile in my left hand . . ." She clapped her hand to her left ear. "Then my private mobile rang. It was my cousin, who sounded upset, and I asked the US negotiator to hold for just half a minute to let me take this other call. Fine, he said, but keep it short, our decision has to be made within a few minutes."

She raised her other hand to the right ear: "My cousin was in tears. Her mother had become ill with fever and diarrhea. My cousin had taken her to an ebola clinic but they couldn't admit anyone, there was a queue already. 'Please, can you help?' So, there I was, with the responsibility for the nation on my left and for my dear aunt on my right," Miatta said.

She fell silent. Her eyes were looking past me with her hands still covering her ears.

I whispered after a while: "What did you choose, your nation or your family?"

Now Miatta looked me in the eye.

"I chose the nation, just as all of us in leadership positions did that autumn. As we did here in the Ministry of Health every single day. During the day, we never stopped working. But at night we wept for the dead, for our friends and colleagues and relatives. Then, slowly, we got the support we needed and began to win against the virus."

I asked the final, necessary question: "What happened to your aunt?"

"She died. It was ebola," Miatta said, as if it had been inevitable.

We were silent for a long while and then I spoke again: "I have been extremely impressed by the work you are all doing. Before I came here, I had accepted what the European media was saying—that the situation was chaotic before international epidemiologists took control."

"Sure. I realize that's how we are portrayed. They are all so crazy about their own organizations. Some of them are great and bring lots of very fine people here to help us. But they want to be praised, the more the better."

She was laughing rather cynically when Luke came in.

"What, are you laughing at me when my back is turned?" he said jokingly.

"No way, we're laughing at the sharks who love being praised," Miatta said happily.

I had already noted that when the leading Liberians felt irritated and exhausted, they used this term for international organizations: "the sharks."

By the beginning of 2015, for the first time since June 2014, fewer than one hundred new confirmed cases were reported in one week for Liberia, Guinea, and Sierra Leone together.

By then, I had returned to the engagements I had put on hold while I went to work on ebola. In January 2015, Agneta and I traveled for a second time to the World Economic Forum in Davos. I was hauling an enormous black suitcase, which was difficult to fit into the luggage compartment on the train.

I was booked to speak in front of a thousand-strong audience in the plenary hall. The presentations from me and Bill and Melinda Gates were to be the first of the main session on Friday night. Our title was *Sustainable Development* and the schedule straightforward: Bill and Melinda Gates would be in conversation about "A Vision for the Future" with the CNN news presenter Fareed Zakaria for about thirty minutes. Before the start of their event, I would have fifteen minutes to speak about "Demystifying the Facts."

Which is where the black suitcase came in.

It was full of audience-response devices, one for each member of the audience. Our plan was to find out what the assembled elite knew about the fundamental facts of today's world. The congress organizers were thrilled. They helped put the devices on the guests' chairs before the doors opened. We at Gapminder had used these devices before to investigate how much particular groups of people knew, and the results had been remarkably disappointing across many different sectors—bankers, politicians, the media and activists at international organizations. Across the board, my lecture audiences tended toward a world view that was thirty years out of date.

This time, though, I thought the results would surely be different. Everyone in that hall was a world leader in his or her field. When I walked out on the stage, I spotted Kofi Annan, the former secretary general of the UN, and his wife in the front row.

I felt quite nervous when I introduced myself.

"I'm going to start by asking you to answer three questions."

The first question came up on the big screen behind me, and then the three multiple choice answers:

During the last twenty years, the proportion of people living in extreme poverty has . . . a) Almost doubled; b) Remained about the same; c) Almost halved.

I watched Kofi Annan as he quickly pressed an answer button. Time for the next question:

How many of the world's one-year-olds are vaccinated against measles? a) Two out of every ten; b) Five out of ten; c) Eight out of ten.

I observed furrowed brows in the hall. My screen showed that the answers were coming in quickly. The technology was working.

I moved on to my last question, which was about the number of children in the world. To illustrate the number, I showed a line graph. In 1950, there had been fewer than 1 billion children and the number had increased steadily until the beginning of the twenty-first century.

What would happen next? The audience saw three options shown as dotted lines: the A line was going up to reach 4 billion children by the year 2100; the B line pointed less steeply upward to 3 billion children; the C line was static, i.e. the number of children would still be 2 billion by the end of the twenty-first century.

This question arguably concerned the world's most fundamental demographic fact.

The audience looked uneasy. Kofi Annan leaned closer to his wife to confer with her. The answers came in more slowly than before but finally everybody had replied.

I showed them how they had done. The question about the proportion of people in extreme poverty had been answered correctly by 61 percent of the Davos delegates—it had been halved in twenty years. Davos delegates had done much better than the Swedish population. Only 23 percent of those polled in Sweden had got the answer right. In the USA, it had been 5 percent.

Then I looked at the question about measles. It was very much an issue of the moment. Many politicians, public-health experts and pharmaceutical-company bosses were in attendance. Besides, Bill and Melinda would soon be speaking on behalf of their foundation, which funded vaccinations for the world's poorest children on a grand scale. I had every reason to assume that the majority of these powerful people would be aware of vaccination rates: more than 80 percent of all one-year-olds.

In fact, only a shockingly low 23 percent of the audience knew the right answer.

What about the demographic question? The right answer is that the number of children is no longer increasing and looks unlikely to change significantly for the rest of this century. The birth rate has stabilized to 130 million children annually because 80 percent of couples worldwide use contraception and the majority of women have access to abortions.

So, how many got this right? Only 26 percent, which is still a whole lot better than people in Sweden and the USA, who managed 11 percent and 8 percent respectively.

I couldn't resist provoking my audience by mentioning the chimpanzees. If chimps in a zoo are offered a choice of bananas marked A, B, or C, they will, by picking randomly, pick each letter 33 percent of the time. Similarly, a group of people with no idea about the right answers could at least be expected to pick correctly one third of the time, just by guessing. This elite audience, after queuing to attend a seminar on socioeconomic and sustainable development, did worse than chimps would on two out of the three questions.

Gapminder's clear, comprehensibly presented data sets have been an amazing success. We have improved the understanding of more than 6 million people every year through discussing our observations in ten TED talks, two BBC documentaries, and many open-access videos and visualization programs. But despite all our efforts to disseminate knowledge, we seemed at best to have had marginal effects on the worldviews of those who were actually meant to know most. This was serious. My questions at Davos were not trivia. They were about fundamental patterns of change in the world.

What is the most accurate way of describing the proportion of extremely poor people: sharply increasing, more or less unchanging or rapidly decreasing? These are radically different alternatives, comparable to basic road sense: is it right to drive when the light is green or yellow or red?

To ask what the proportion is of all one-year-olds who have been vaccinated against measles is the equivalent of asking what the proportion is of all children who have access to basic healthcare. Any answer other than 80 percent reveals that you are thirty years behind your time.

Anyone who does not know that most people have access to contraception and that the total number of children worldwide is no longer increasing has failed to grasp essential demographic facts.

When I returned to Stockholm, I told Ola and Anna that not even the Davos delegates knew the facts about the world, a world that classed them as very important people. We agreed it was time to change our approach. My conclusion was that we should try to produce better teaching material, but Ola and Anna disagreed. Anna stressed that what we had was already very good. Something else was needed. Perhaps the public and the experts in "the old West" were all psychologically blocked when it came to having a realistic understanding of "the other world." Our new job had to be to grab people's attention and make them understand what makes ignorance so persistent.

A little later, Ola and Anna formulated a concept: "Factfulness."

We made it the title of our book and began at once to set out our thoughts.

Afterword
by Fanny Härgestam

"Hans Rosling is going to write a book. Would you like to give him a hand?"

The question was put to me by the publisher at Natur & Kultur, Richard Herold, who phoned me one evening in December 2016. I took the call standing on a metro platform. The book was not to be just about Hans's work, as with *Factfulness*, the book they had already started on. Instead, it would tell the story of his life. The project was urgent, Richard said, explaining that Hans was seriously ill with cancer and might not have much time left. The writing had to be done at speed.

It soon became clear that Hans had already begun a memoir. It was a text fragment he had written during the last few months, and it needed reworking and extending.

A couple of weeks later, Richard and I went to Uppsala and stood waiting outside Hans and Agneta's door. We had brought a bag of muffins for this first encounter. Maybe the only one. When we pressed the doorbell, I felt nervous. What to expect? Is he bedridden? Will he be able to speak?

Agneta opened the door and then Hans bustled in, smiling delightedly. He had no problem talking, that much was instantly obvious. We stood inspecting the different objects in the hall for quite a while as Hans enthusiastically told us their stories, one by one.

Among other things, there was a huge, red wooden clock placed inside a huge, red wooden crib next to two red wooden chairs. The

By the clock

whole arrangement, which took up a lot of space, was an artwork awarded to Hans. The hall was the only space where it would fit.

A map on the wall showed Agneta's family farm in Vassunda, now turned into a golf course. "You know where it is, don't you?" he asked and looked at me.

It was like a little test and it amused Hans. I admitted that my grasp of the local geography of Uppsala County was pretty feeble, but he probably didn't hear me because he was already on his way into the sitting room while telling us about how he and Agneta had just celebrated fifty years together as a couple.

"If you are secure in a relationship you are set free to move in space and thought," he said.

When they were fourteen, Agneta and Hans were in the same class at school. One of their teachers had pointed out that, statistically, some people in the class would get married to each other. Agneta remembers scanning her classmates and thinking: "Not me, at any rate." Just a couple of years later, Agneta and Hans met at a New Year celebration—an anything-but-sober party at the Temperance Society in Uppsala. They have been partners ever since.

Once we were all in the sitting room, Agneta served coffee while Hans handed us copies of his CV, neatly prepared on two sheets of paper stapled together. He clearly wasn't very willing to speak about his illness and preferred the subject of "the world."

He had pulled out the dining table near the seating area to have his laptop close at hand.

"Watch out, lots of cables everywhere," he said as he ferreted about under the table with the remote in one hand.

As dusk gathered around Uppsala, he spoke to the graphs of child mortality, gesticulating in front of the screen with his thin arms. Before I could follow how he did it, the numbers and the graphs were turning into anecdotes. After filling our coffee cups, Hans told us about his time as a young medic working in a hospital in Mozambique in the 1970s. Richard and I listened in silence. He spoke in particular about the hard decisions he had faced and described having to cut unborn babies into pieces to be able to extract them and save the mother's life. It was extreme poverty that created such impossible dilemmas. He said that working in low-income countries had often frustrated him to the point that he feared he'd go mad. His years of research in Africa had been tough and his workload had sometimes coincided with personal tragedies affecting him and his family. He spoke of seeing mothers lose their children and knowing the pain they suffered because he had felt it, too, when he and Agneta lost their daughter.

Agneta added to the narrative now and then. It had grown dark outside when the words began to flow more slowly. Suddenly, his voice broke. Tears ran down his cheeks. Agneta wept with him. They were controlled and quiet, sitting closely together on the sofa.

"It has been a long time since either of us talked about this," Hans said.

I got my first email from Hans later that evening. He said he felt somehow re-ignited despite his illness. From then onward, we were in touch by email or phone practically every day. If I went traveling, I took the tape deck and the tapes of our conversations. I always recorded our conversations.

He sent a photo of himself one afternoon with the caption "Great pose if one wants to come across as fit": he had been snapped on a cross-country skiing trek.

Hans seemed healthy and alert at our meetings, which often lasted for hours. Meeting to talk had become part of our routine. We might start in the morning, carry on until a midday break and then speak all afternoon. Hans always sounded eager when he took a call.

"We'll start from the beginning," he often said, when realizing that he had shot off into a discourse that had nothing whatever to do with our main subject.

While Hans was writing new parts of his memoirs, I worked on the existing text to find passages I would like to reshape or rewrite in greater depth. I always asked him what he thought. He was eager for me to understand him and his background but he also wanted to tell me about how he saw the world.

"It will be a kind of crash course in world development for you, Fanny," he used to say. I imagined him smiling contentedly on the other end of the phone as I asked him follow-up questions about vaccine availability or the links between freedom of expression and economic development.

We discussed the direction of the book many times and at great length. He tended to look for conclusions and argued like the born pedagogue he was, asking questions like: "What will the reader learn by reading this chapter?" For my part, I tried all the time to find out about his past experiences, and how Hans had been affected personally by different events; but it could be tricky to make him focus on a particular moment.

When he did open up, however, he did so unguardedly, without reservations. He had wept spontaneously that first day we met in Uppsala, just as he later could become emotional when recalling other things that had happened in his past and people he had met.

Hans worried that his own life and his thoughts on what his social background signified would not add up to anything of sufficient interest. He also worried about time being too short.

"There are so many stories I'd like to tell," he often said.

I tried in vain to persuade him that his first concern was groundless. As for the second one, I shared it—time was short.

We didn't make it.

"I'll get back to you when I'm in a fit state to talk again," he wrote in his last text message to me. He died three days later.

I was able to complete his memoirs mainly because of the hours of interviews with Hans that I had taped in January and early February 2017. I read a lot by Hans's own hand, all the articles, lecture notes and interview transcripts. To complete the narrative and fill in details of his accounts, I carried out additional interviews with people who knew Hans professionally as well as privately.

Talking with Agneta was a special part of my preparations for the book. She illustrated her stories by showing me photos from their travels and jobs as well as their day-to-day life together. Hans had been a father and a spouse, sides of him that I learned little about from him, but which, after his death, emerged from the stories told by Agneta and their children.

Agneta and I spent a few days together in the southern province of Skåne in the summer of 2017. We went down to the beach, with its strong winds and warm sand, wrapped in the striped terry-gowns I had seen hung on the wall of the upstairs landing in the small, white-rendered house that had been passed on to Agneta. In the summers, generations of her family have been coming to stay in this traditional cottage.

The summers are often cool but, regardless, Agneta walks every morning along the narrow path to the sea and—if the water is at least 55 degrees—goes for a swim. She and Hans came here often and, during their last few years together, talked about moving in for good. Hans enjoyed the seaside but, unlike Agneta, wasn't too keen on getting into the water. He walked to the beach fully dressed, in shirt, trousers, socks, and sandals. This was his favorite activity, to walk along the beach where the sea meets the sand.

"Still, I got him to swim as far as the jetty over there," Agneta said, pointing at a small jetty, which one could dive from, a bit farther along.

Nearby, a stream wound its way to the sea, making loops in the sand. Small children were playing in the shallow pools.

Every summer, Hans would set to work to dam the stream. He looked forward to his project, which had no purpose other

Damming the stream in Svarte

than keeping him amused. His goal was to change the direction of the stream by building a dam with boulders and sand shoveled on at top speed. He recruited family and strangers alike as stone-carrying slaves. His own task was to plan the new estuary and he would be very pleased if the wind was helpful. On really good days, the wind changed direction so that the stream shifted position naturally.

Hans had chemotherapy treatment during his last summer but felt reasonably well: a little more breathless than usual but happy to go swimming now and then. The two of them had agreed to live as normally as possible, taking daily walks and starting the day with cheese sandwiches for breakfast in the untamed garden.

Indoors, there was a desk in every room, ready for Hans to settle down. He usually preferred to write upstairs in a room with a view over the apple trees.

"He had realized the time to sum up had come. To focus on what had been, rather than what the future might bring," Agneta said.

It was something he had not given himself time to do before. The process of "summing up" absorbed him, but Agneta saw to it that he left his desk to move about or come downstairs for meals. If she hadn't strong-armed him, he would have done neither.

"He wasn't always the easiest man to coach," Agneta said with a smile. She coached him, yes, but she drove herself, too. "I never agreed just to accompany Hans on his travels. My condition was that I would be part of the plan in my own right."

They were driven by the same ideals and shared fundamental values. Many have wondered how Agneta endured Hans's relentless intensity. But they were actually very much like each other.

During their last Skåne summer together, they often spoke about their gratitude: "We had much to be grateful for. We understood very well how rich our lives had been. And we had been given opportunities to see so much of the world together."

Even as the cancer weakened Hans, his talent for, and love of, talking didn't fade.

"He began to talk the moment he opened his eyes in the morning. No one had a chance to get a word in first. It was no use trying to silence him. He'd just carry on, homing in on another angle," Agneta remembered.

She smiled absently, looking out over the sea.

Hans could slip into lecturing mode at the family dinner and, once engaged in his own line of argument, block queues at buffet tables and stop everyone from getting at the food.

While the children were still living with their parents, they had a rota for doing household chores. It was very clear about Hans's responsibilities. It meant that the Rosling home didn't always have a clean kitchen worktop and so forth—but that was all right. Agneta never expected them to approach domestic issues in the same way.

She was just as tolerant about his periods of parental leave. When Hans was at home looking after their eldest daughter, Anna, when she was a baby, he was reading the Russian writer Aleksandr Solzhenitsyn. Anna liked biscuits and crawling, so Hans kept her happily occupied by throwing biscuits around the room. He could read a few more lines while she crawled off to find the next biscuit. Similarly, when he was caring for their youngest son, Magnus, the toddler had taken a fancy to the contents of the wastepaper basket. To keep Magnus happy, Hans emptied out the scrunched-up paper on the floor. Meanwhile, Daddy got on with writing his thesis.

Agneta shrugged when she recalled those episodes: "Whatever, it worked both for him and the children."

It was during this time in their lives that Hans decided the children's core diet should be porridge. He had taken on board that children need to eat something around five o'clock every evening. Fixing a pot of porridge was easy, and to amuse everyone he gave it a stylish name: "oat flake soufflé." It came in four basic varients: normal, burned, salted, and unsalted. The kids only protested if he forgot the salt.

Hans would frequently lose items of clothing. Every year, Hans usually lost articles of outdoor clothing more than once. Agneta's policy was to buy mega-packs of identical woolly hats and gloves that the whole family could use. Once, Hans had to collect his heavy outdoor shoes from the headquarters of the Security Service. He had been to a meeting at the prime minister's country residence, forgotten all about his boots and traveled home wearing his best indoor shoes. It took a year before he found the time to collect them.

As the house husband, he could still be effectively absent. When he was preoccupied with his own concerns, the family freezer was easily emptied of ice creams. As happened the time Ola and Anna came home from primary school together and politely asked for an ice cream each. "Sure thing," Hans said, intent on what he was writing. A little later, the kids turned up again and asked for ice creams. Same reply. This ran on repeat until Hans was told that there were none left. He was baffled.

Hans never felt hungry but if he calculated that an energy boost was needed to stay up reading, he would eat granulated sugar straight from the bag.

He could seem invulnerable because the opinions of others didn't hurt him. He didn't really worry about being thought irritating. But if the egocentric side of Hans often caught attention, he also had a powerful, perceptive interest in understanding people's needs.

At the end of the summer of Hans's last year of life, Anna and her family were planning to move to the USA. He was already unwell and Anna agonized: should they go or stay? It was hard for her. She thought maybe moving would be best, after all, and sat down with her father to talk about it, listing the advantages and disadvantages of the two options.

His first impulse had been to ask her to stay but, he said, he had decided ignore it. After thinking things over, he told her that they should of course go. They were not to hang about in Sweden, just waiting for him to die.

"Hans has always been instinctively cautious. Looking back, you might have thought him something of a daredevil, but he wasn't, not at all. He found out what the circumstances were and came to considered conclusions," Agneta said, while poking at the logs in the open hearth.

One prospect frightened Hans: that of his children or grandchildren somehow being hurt.

"If you ever think that going someplace on a motorbike is a good idea—don't. Take a taxi and I'll pay the difference," he said to Magnus, who went to Beijing for a year's study after finishing senior school. All motorbike driving was forbidden. "And don't walk city streets if you're drunk," he might say. "You'll get mugged."

Hans laid down few rules but didn't mince words. Wrapping things up wasn't his style. When Anna wanted to stay the night in a youth hostel—she was in her early teens—he told her to come and have a word with him in his "office." Actually, his office was a cubbyhole in the cellar, originally intended for a sauna, with just enough room for a desk and a chair. Hans had taken the chair's armrests off to be able to wriggle into the seat. Crammed into the office, Anna got a lecture on safe sex. Hans added a few words of comfort: if she got pregnant, he and Agneta would obviously take care of the baby so that Anna could finish her education. A baby would be no problem. The serious issue was risking HIV infection.

Anna was flustered. She explained to her dad that they were getting together to watch Monty Python films and eat hot dogs.

When the children were in their teens, Hans did a deal with them. If they needed to be collected from somewhere, they could phone him at any time. He'd drive them. But they must call. In return, the children had to promise to visit Hans in his elderly care home, when the time came.

During Anna's years in middle and senior school, Hans acted as driver for her and her friends most Saturdays and Sundays, because he was always sober, alert, and ready to go. He had little need of creature comforts and would often be up at all hours, working or playing with a flight simulator program. Besides, he thought it good fun to fit Anna and her girlfriends into all available spaces of the white family Volvo. As their driver, he was quiet and pretended not to be there. He like listening to the girls discussing the evening and their youthful thoughts about life and everything.

After one of Magnus's far-too-wild nights on the town, Hans picked him up without a word of admonition. Instead, he brought a thermos of coffee.

The door to the Rosling home was always open. It often filled with visitors. The children's friends came and went, ate with the family, and slept over. They were all quizzed at the table by Hans, whose curiosity was ever active, in his everyday life as well as at work. Young people intrigued him; he wanted to know where they came from and what they thought. His African postgraduate students would be invited round, especially at Christmas and to receptions and birthday parties. They were guests at these parties because, as Hans said, it would interest them to see what Swedish home life was like. In return, he liked to seek out his students when they were working elsewhere in Europe. He would arrange to visit them, often in the summer, when the Rosling family set out on their annual camping holiday.

Hans, Agneta, and the children would roam around the European continent in their white Volvo, packed to the rafters and with a roof box on top. Hans always brought at least one suitcase full of unread academic literature, but often got sucked into a doorstop-size novel. They camped and changed site daily,

On skis

sleeping in a green tent bought from a classified ad. It ranked as "Eastern Europe's ugliest," said Agneta, "the kind of tent everyone had stopped using."

Hans collected countries. When all the bigger ones had been ticked off the list, they went for the smaller and the more distant territories—Andorra, Monaco, and so on. They were not allowed to put a tick against a country until they had eaten something there. They carried a gas-fired camping stove but meals were never great performances in the Rosling family. Eating amounted to fuel provision, to keep you going, and bread was as good as anything. Agneta fixed herself cups of instant coffee in the boot of the car—except for the year when Hans forgot the stove, but managed to pack a portable fax machine. "His mind prioritized his paperwork above our family packing," Agneta commented.

The grass is still damp after the rain but the garden sofa and chairs are dry. We are sitting together, Agneta and I, in what she calls their "OAP incubator": a garden folly built from wood and glass. Multicolored paper lanterns hang from the ceiling and a standard lamp, all askew and wrapped in its flex, stands in a corner. Agneta lays the table with colorful tea mugs and a tin of digestive biscuits. Then she puts her glasses on and opens up her laptop to show her large collection of photos.

"Look, here we are in Nacala," she says, poring over a black-and-white picture. "There must've been a power cut because it's raining but we're busy lighting a fire outside."

In the autumn of 2016, Hans had a full schedule even though he had canceled all his speaking engagements. He was especially preoccupied with the writing of *Factfulness*, the book he was working on together with Ola and Anna. Sorting his papers and old photographs for his memoirs also took a lot of time. He worked full-time during the periods when he felt well enough, writing passages and always trying to be precise about names and places. Sometimes he became nostalgic, but never self-destructively so. Rooting about in the boxes full of letters and notes in the attic fascinated him. He had saved everything and often talked to his family about how hard it was to recall the order of past events.

He also immersed himself in understanding his type of cancer and would inform Agneta about his latest reading. Hans, as always, grew utterly absorbed in this new subject and sometimes knew more about it than the doctors who looked after him. He and Agneta had decided not to give up, and lived as if there would be a solution—a cure. Agneta concentrated on trying to get him to eat and enjoy himself a little, despite everything.

Throughout his life, he seems to have bothered as little with rest as with food. He would never just lie back on a sofa: he had to learn to do so during his last year. He kept checking the step-counter on his mobile phone until the end. "Better do a few laps now," he'd say, and do the rounds of the hall and the kitchen.

Later that evening, we set out in the car to the small fishing village of Abbekås. The idea is to have supper in the harbor pub. As we drive between the wide Skåne plains and the sea, the waves have white crests and the sky is covered in dark clouds. The harbor pub is almost full. Two men are playing guitar and singing songs.

Agneta and Hans often came here for their evening meal. Their usual small table was discreetly close to a wall and Hans would sit with his back to the room in order not to be recognized. He even refrained from asking the staff about their life histories. This was perhaps the one place where his curiosity was tempered by his wish to be left in peace.

At all other times, Hans would talk to people he met, regardless of whether it was on the beach at Svarte, at the World Economic Forum in Davos or in the Nacala hospital. He was driven by a need to understand how people felt and thought, and how things functioned, and never gave in until he thought he had got it. The will to change followed the reaching of an understanding—that sums up how he saw his life's task.

Agneta tells an anecdote from their time in Mozambique. The story began when a couple who lived nearby knocked on their door. The neighbors were poor. Their home, a little farther down the road, was a simple shed with three walls and a roof. The wife had just given birth, and afterward she and her husband kept in touch with Hans and Agneta, who had both advised her to take contraceptive pills, which were supplied free of charge.

Now the couple wanted to let the doctor know that it was not like he thought, because the pills were not free and they couldn't afford the price. The pharmacist wanted to be paid, they said. Apparently, the Nacala pharmacist was running a private black market in contraceptive pills. Hans immediately started an investigation and it turned out that several members of the hospital staff had heard the rumor—the pharmacist was lining his own pockets at the patients' expense.

Hans, who had trusted the pharmacist, kick-started a long process of stopping this trade. Hardly any wrongdoing angered him more than someone putting obstacles in the way of public health measures. Agneta remembered when Hans came home one evening, cursing "that crook," and swore he'd get him locked up. He got there in the end: the police arrested and charged the pharmacist, who was sentenced to prison.

Later, Agneta and Hans laughed at the whole wretched episode, but it could happen that Hans sighed and felt dejected.

Deep down, though, he never gave up.

When the workload was heavy, he urged people around him on with the cry: "Advance into the night!"

When progress seemed hopeless, he often said with a smile: "It's never too late to give in, so we might as well do it some other time!"

Appendix: On Cassava

Perhaps Hans Rosling's most significant discovery in his field of research was his explanation of konzo, an illness with lower-limb paralysis as its main symptom. He showed that the illness arose in regions of severe malnutrition and was caused by a monotonous diet consisting of poorly prepared cassava.

Here, Linley Chiwona-Karltun, who did her doctoral research under Hans Rosling's supervision, explains aspects of the crop that are crucial for understanding its effects.

Cassava has many other names, including manioc. It is a drought-tolerant root crop, which grows well in poor soils and is the main source of carbohydrates for people living in sub-Saharan Africa. It is native to South America, where it was first cultivated. Portuguese explorers introduced the plant into West Africa in the sixteenth century and by the twentieth century it had spread widely.

The starchy cassava roots store more carbohydrate per hectare than any other crop. The leaves can be boiled and provide an important source of proteins, vitamins, and minerals.

Cassava is classified as either "sweet-cool" or "bitter"; the bitter variety is poisonous, the sweet one less so, and edible without prior cooking. Bitter cassava contains cyanogenic glucosides in much higher concentration than the sweet type, and these substances become further concentrated in drought conditions. The plants also contain an enzyme that can break down the glucosides and eventually generate free hydrogen cyanide. Bitter cassava must be carefully processed before eating: the enzyme must have time to do its job. Afterward, the hydrogen cyanide must be washed away. In practice, the roots are soaked, grated or fermented, and then either dried in the sun or roasted before cooking. The detoxification process can take between three and fourteen days.

In dry areas such as the Mozambican plateau near Nacala, lack of water makes drying in the sun the only possible method. That form of processing takes several weeks.

At times when cassava is the most important source of energy, the growers normally prefer to cultivate the toxic varieties, because of their bigger yields and high tolerance to poor soils and little or no rain. The poisons are protective against crop theft by monkeys and men. The growers are usually women, who have learned to distinguish between plants with low and high toxicity, and tend to surround patches of sweet cassava with rows of the bitter type.

During field studies in Malawi, Hans and I studied these women's knowledge about the different cassava varieties. When we asked them just how bitter and poisonous they were, the woman would show us by pointing at the root to indicate just how much of it you could eat without becoming ill. We were later able to prove in the laboratory that they knew exactly what they were talking about.

Linley Chiwona-Karltun